12/97

INNOVATION

Breakthrough Thinking at
3M, DuPont, GE,
Pfizer, and Rubbermaid

INNOVATION

Breakthrough Thinking at 3M, DuPont, GE, Pfizer, and Rubbermaid

EDITED BY

ROSABETH MOSS KANTER

JOHN KAO

FRED WIERSEMA

HarperBusiness

A Division of HarperCollinsPublishers

INNOVATION. Copyright © 1997 by Wordworks, Inc. All rights reserved. Printed in the United States of America. No part of this book may be used or reproduced in any manner whatsoever without written permission except in the case of brief quotations embodied in critical articles and reviews. For information address HarperCollins Publishers, Inc., 10 East 53rd Street, New York, NY 10022.

HarperCollins books may be purchased for educational, business, or sales promotional use. For information please write: Special Markets Department, HarperCollins Publishers, Inc., 10 East 53rd Street, New York, NY 10022.

FIRST EDITION

Designed by Jessica Shatan

Library of Congress Cataloging-in-Publication Data

Innovation : breakthrough thinking at 3M, DuPont, GE, Pfizer, and
    Rubbermaid / edited by Rosabeth Moss Kanter, John Kao, and Fred
    Wiersema ; foreword by Tom Peters. — 1st ed.
        p.   cm. — (BusinessMasters series)
    Includes index.
    ISBN 0-88730-771-X
    1. Technological innovations—United States—Management—Case
studies.   2. Manufactures—United States—Technological innovations—
Management—Case studies.   3. New Products—United States—
Management—Case studies.   I. Kanter, Rosabeth Moss.   II. Kao, John J.
III. Wiersema, Frederik D. (Frederik Derk)   IV. Series.
HD45.I53726   1997
658.5'14—dc21   97-7138

97 98 99 00 01 ❖/RRD 10 9 8 7 6 5 4 3 2 1

Contents

Foreword

Companies that thrive on chaos by constant innovation are the only ones set to survive in the years to come. Most people I talk to say they support innovators. They admire them and reward them. But most of those windbags get sweaty palms when it comes to betting bucks on the bay (read: market redefiners). They're happier to watch their well-trained, well-fed, obedient little ponies trotting around their R&D paddocks (read: line extensions).

David Friend, founder of Pilot Software, makers of information-access tools used by large companies, frequently lectures on innovation at MIT's Sloan School of Management. People, he says, have a tough time getting comfortable with innovation. Why? Because they can't imagine an immediate and tangible return on their investment. They want quantifiable results; they want to invest in sure sales, steady returns, and satisfied customers. They want 2:1 odds, not 50:1.

At Pfizer Pharmaceuticals, one of the five companies featured in *Business Masters: Innovation*, the R&D gang proposes literally thousands of ideas for new drugs. Out of every hundred, only half are considered worthy of pursuing to the development stage. After a second cut, only ten make it to the processing stage. Out of those ten, only *one* makes it through the required tests, protocols, and approvals to arrive on the shelves of our local pharmacies. And talk about venturing forth when the return on innovation is invisible! The process that takes a typical pharmaceutical from abstract concept to marketable reality can take up to fifteen capital-devouring years!

Few companies have the stomach for such delayed gratification. Pfizer and the other four companies in this book customarily take monetary risks that would give most corporate finance officers advanced cases of indigestion. These companies spend in the neighborhood of $1 billion a year on research and development. At Pfizer, that amounts to upwards of 17 percent of gross sales.

What does it take to be a master of innovation? As the top executives from 3M, DuPont, General Electric, Pfizer, and Rubbermaid tell us, innovation does not come cheap. Nor does it come easy. You can't just hire the winner of the local science and technology fair, give her an assignment, and expect her to come up with the next big thing . . . now.

More often than not, innovation is slow *and* painful.

P-e-r-i-o-d.

At DuPont, for example, it can take as many as *two hundred fifty* raw ideas to yield *one* major marketable product. Think about that, please:

$$250 \text{ RIs} = 1 \text{ MP}$$
Equation

Or, to put it another way, if you hired one thousand top research scientists and locked them away in a laboratory equipped with top-notch gizmos and a steady supply of fast food, you might reasonably expect them to come up with a winner 0.4 percent of the time. Or as our colleague in the pharmaceutical business put it, "Most scientists do not produce over one winner in the course of an entire career, but that doesn't mean they're lousy scientists."

Small wonder that Joseph Miller, senior vice president of research and development at DuPont, says that innovation is actually "risk management." If you're committed to innovation, you've got to have a very high tolerance for risk *and* failure.

As these R&D champs teach us, even the certainty of failure must not jeopardize an innovator's potential for success. At 3M, managers have adopted the 15 percent rule: 3M's folks can devote up to 15 percent of their time to projects of their own choosing, *without seeking approval from above or even bothering to tell managers what it is they are working on!*

I *love* that! 3M also cultivates an atmosphere where ideas flow from one division to the next, rarely meeting a barrier or being blocked by corporate politics. As a result, the stellar firm now boasts an arsenal of some fifty thousand products ranging from masking tape to microreplication technology.

You can try to achieve such diversity by buying up every new company on the block, or you can develop it from scratch and from within by freeing up your people to work wherever their creative energies take them. 3M unmistakably chooses the latter course.

To achieve such elevated levels of innovation, you've got to have a deep trust in your people (and they in you). That doesn't mean you should splinter every performance yardstick, ignore crucial business needs, and give people free rein to gallop off in any direction they damn well please. Each of the business masters profiled in this book creates "stretch" programs and performance targets. And even Triple Crown winners appreciate a healthy carrot of prespecified length at the end of the stick.

At 3M, this comes in the form of the 30/4 rule: 30 percent of sales *must* come from products no less than four years old.

I, for one, love to watch these business masters at full throttle, racing to a finish line that can never be reached. Thoroughbreds, whether in nature or in business, are both born *and* made. The right genes—a corporate culture that enshrines flexibility and puts hard money behind innovation—may be in place, but that's still no promise you'll get to wear the roses, or for that matter, that you'll not eventually get sent to the glue factory. You've got to be willing to handle a long and challenging track, look unfrowningly on frequent failures, and trust that the occasional serendipitous dis-covery will prod movement in an idea that was stuck at the starting gate.

Tomorrow's victories will go to the masters of innovation! Period!

TOM PETERS

Editors' Note

In today's business world, few words are thrown around with quite as much abandon as *innovation*. Yet few concepts are as misunderstood. Too many managers still view innovation with suspicion, as the exclusive province of R&D, of dreamers and inventors. They have no faith that it can be practiced in recruiting and hiring, purchasing, and finance—indeed in every unit and department of a company. Too often innovation is viewed as a one-shot deal, a quick injection of new ideas or process improvements designed to shake up the status quo. In fact, innovation should be systematic and perpetual, built into a company's culture and processes. We hope this book can clarify some of these misconceptions and demonstrate how five great companies have turned themselves into integrated innovation machines.

3M, DuPont, General Electric, Pfizer, and Rubbermaid are among the proudest names in world business. Each has proven itself a leader year after year, decade after decade. Each has found a way to institutionalize innovation, to take it out of the realm of the theoretical and turn it into a practical tool of business success.

For over ninety-five years, 3M has been making superior products for our homes, offices, and communities—everything from Scotch tape to Thinsulate. The company has a long-standing reputation as a progressive, quality-obsessed organization committed to the welfare of its people. In recent years, 3M has become a powerhouse of integrated innovation. Every employee is a fully empowered idea scout. 3M's 15 percent solution is a model for companies worldwide: Employees are expected to spend 15 percent of their time on self-directed projects. They are free to use company resources without first garnering approval from above. The result: sky-high morale and a continuous stream of innovative products.

DuPont is well known for its extraordinary contributions to human welfare in the fields of chemistry. Its R&D department is a model of how an unstinting commitment of resources and talent can lead to revolutionary scientific progress. However, innovation does not stop at the laboratory door; it is pervasive throughout the company. To keep its employees abreast of developments in their fields, the company has over three hundred topic-specific networks linking colleagues around the world. In the field of human resources, DuPont's pioneer Just-In-Time Care program allows employees with home and family issues to receive comprehensive counseling and referrals. The result: a marked increase in morale and company loyalty.

General Electric is one of the most familiar and trusted brand names in the world. For generations, American households have proudly used GE products. But, like many older companies, GE stagnated in the 1970s. More recently, under Jack Welch's inspired leadership, it has become the very model of a perpetual innovation machine—and the world's most profitable company. GE has set itself the goal of becoming a boundaryless organization, one in which cooperation and innovation flow without impediment throughout the organization. The company's Work-Out sessions, free-wheeling discussion groups, allow people to express their ideas and opinions. The result: innovative suggestions from unexpected quarters and increased across-the-board productivity.

Since 1849, Pfizer has been one of the world's proudest names in pharmaceuticals. Its products have enhanced and extended the lives of millions of people. Yet Pfizer is hardly resting on its laurels. It has entered the Information Age with a vengeance. The company has built one of the world's premier knowledge-gathering systems. Whether a project succeeds or fails, all insights become part of the company's vast knowledge bank, readily available across the organization.

Pfizer understands and harnesses the power of learning. The result: less duplicated work, speedier decision-making, a profound depth and breadth of collective knowledge.

Rubbermaid is a part of all our daily lives. Its superbly designed products make routine household chores a little bit easier. This is a company that never stands still. It funds R&D with a virtual blank check and reveres creativity and technological innovation. When the price of resin, the primary component of most of its products, went up, the company refused to cut R&D for a quick bottom-line fix. The result: long-term strength and the ability to introduce literally hundreds of new and improved products annually.

Obviously, the five companies profiled in this book are not the only innovators out there. However, they were chosen because they have succeeded in inculcating innovation into the very fibers of their organizations. To these winners, there is nothing intangible or amorphous about innovation. It is a practical way to ensure the long-term health of their enterprises—for customers, employees, and communities. In fact, the five companies have been doing just that for a combined total of a remarkable 626 years. Clearly, there is much all of us can learn from their examples.

—ROSABETH MOSS KANTER,
JOHN KAO,
FRED WIERSEMA

May 1997

The Editors on Innovation

In reading the case studies in this book, we realized anew how crucial and comprehensive innovation has become in today's economy. We realized, too, that innovation demands perpetual learning: it is, by definition, a state of continuous flux. In order to share our latest thoughts on the subject and hopefully learn from one another, we hit upon the idea of holding a free-flowing roundtable discussion. Our goal was to share knowledge and perhaps trigger some fresh insights. We hope you will find the results as intriguing and beneficial as we did, that your imaginations will be stimulated, and that you'll consider holding similar discussions within your own companies.

JOHN KAO: I'm always asked, "What are the rules for innovation?" That's like asking, "What are the rules for formulating a strategy?" There are no hard-and-fast rules. In business, as in art, the only true measure is: Does it work?

The five companies in this book employ a wide range of techniques to foster and sustain innovation. The key is to understand what a company needs in terms of its product, industry, leadership, and culture.

FRED WIERSEMA: What's really fascinating is how certain companies, even after they become monstrously large, are able to remain innovative—year after year, decade after decade.

ROSABETH KANTER: A universal characteristic of innovative companies is an open culture. A culture that reaches out to relationships in all directions: across functions and departments internally, and with every potentially beneficial external connection.

JOHN KAO: There are a lot of relationships that companies traditionally haven't even thought about. The concept of alumni networks is one. If you can create a company that is exciting and nurturing, that is a place where people grow and prosper, they'll want to stay in touch even after they leave. This creates a vast information infrastructure that enlarges your reach. Goodwill is something you can't put a dollar sign on, but in many cases it leads to knowledge-sharing and accelerated innovation.

ROSABETH KANTER: I'm often asked what the first step is toward creating a challenging, innovative environment.

Don't try to mastermind it from the top. Put together a team of your most talented people. Give them a mission: to make the company a more exciting place to work. Unleash their creativity. They'll come back to you with dozens of ideas, and some will be brilliant. Ask for company-wide input on these ideas. You're liberating people's imaginations. That in itself creates a more challenging environment—and a momentum is started.

JOHN KAO: Be prepared for a lot of conflict. Innovation is messy. There's a constantly shifting set of agendas. It's very difficult to manage. Even companies with long histories of successful innovation sometimes fall on their faces. You have to understand cycles and respond accordingly. You have to balance the needs of your established fair-haired child and your wailing infant. The demands on leadership are enormous. You won't find the answers in a procedure manual.

ROSABETH KANTER: There's a tendency to romanticize innovation—to think it's synonymous with intuition and inspiration. Wrong. Innovation requires an incredible amount of sheer brain power. Intellectual smarts. An ability to hold more than one idea in your head at the same time, to understand contradiction, to listen to many voices. The leaders who get into trouble are the ones who get lucky—and then don't realize it was luck. They think they know more than anyone else. Ken Olsen at Digital is a prime example. He didn't listen when his people told him personal computers were the next stage. Mistake of historic proportions. Leaders have to let themselves be challenged.

FRED WIERSEMA: And they have to get out of the way. Innovation rarely happens at the core. It happens on the fringes, in out-of-the-way places, away from the dampening influences of bureaucracy and politics. To complicate matters, as a company grows, the core becomes increasingly powerful. One of the big challenges is to keep the margins alive.

ROSABETH KANTER: If a project is highly innovative, outside the company's mainstream, then it's going to need protective shielding because people are going to find a lot of reasons to shoot it down.

JOHN KAO: I agree about protecting a project from slings and arrows. I call it woodshedding. The jazz great Charlie Parker went to the woodshed behind his house and experimented with new scales for years. He didn't want premature criticism or praise. He simply wanted the freedom to experiment. 3M is masterful at keeping its edges percolating with new ideas.

FRED WIERSEMA: 3M's 15 percent rule is one of the great innovations in and of itself. The rule states that 15 percent of every employee's time should be spent on self-directed projects. That sends a strong message that ideas are respected and that risk-taking is not only condoned but expected.

JOHN KAO: It's more a cultural value, an ideological statement, than a management control mechanism per se. It's not about time cards. It's about demonstrating that 3M values unallocated time and blank conceptual space.

FRED WIERSEMA: On a practical level, the company is approving use of its resources to work on projects they haven't even considered yet.

JOHN KAO: The rule allows someone to tinker with an off-the-wall project his supervisor might not understand. It equalizes the equation. Your boss can't tell you what to do more than 85 percent of the time.

ROSABETH KANTER: There's more to innovation than projects and products.

FRED WIERSEMA: Good point. Look at what Sam Walton did. The success of Wal-Mart has virtually nothing to do with product development. It's based on innovation in processes such as supplier relationships, distribution, location, and pricing.

ROSABETH KANTER: And in the very concept of what the business is. Wal-Mart basically reinvented American retailing. In most companies, there's abundant room for innovation. In the rush to bring out new products, support functions are often shortchanged. Markets are growing increasingly volatile, and to keep up, companies have to embrace integrated change across their organizations—and beyond.

FRED WIERSEMA: The innovation process has three major components. The first is invention—getting ideas. The second is development—turning ideas into reality. This stage calls for extraordinary discipline and focus. The third stage is getting the product on the market and making it a huge success. This stage—which includes distribution, pricing, marketing, and public relations—demands integration. The best companies forge electronic links between suppliers, distributors, and customers. Setting up this complex and instantly responsive system requires a whole different set of skills than the first two stages.

Each of these three major components has a different set of criteria. One of the first things a company should do is take an innovation inventory: assess its strengths and weaknesses at each stage. It's also crucial to understand how willing, ready, and able your people are. Stimulating individual innovation is a challenge in itself. Turning your entire company into a perpetual innovation machine is obviously far more complex. It requires a tremendous amount of organizational discipline.

ROSABETH KANTER: One of the problems in certain highly creative organizations, including many high-tech companies, is that they place too much emphasis on the first stage. They're very good at invention but lack the discipline needed to bring their ideas to market quickly. Sometimes they're unable to sustain manufacturing excellence.

Fred's point about integrated, holistic innovation is an important one. I always ask people what historic innovations they associate with General Motors. Most mention products or technology. Occasionally somebody will bring up color, because GM was the first automaker to offer different color cars. But the example that I always use is consumer finance. If GM hadn't invented consumer credit, nobody would have been able to buy their cars. It's an example of an innovation that supports a company's ability to carry out its core mission. More recently, look at what GM has done with Saturn. It has reinvented the dealer organization, the treatment of customers, and methods for delivering cars. Again, these are secondary functions that support the core product. Similarly, Merck's innovative recruiting, hiring, and benefits practices support its ability to attract and retain highly talented people.

FRED WIERSEMA: GE is a prime example of integrated innovation. Fifteen years ago, Jack Welch came in, cut through the politics and bureaucracy, and focused like a laser on producing quality products. He quickly realized that the distribution process was a mess. It's no good to have terrific products if they don't reach the market quickly and efficiently. Welch restructured all of GE's support functions, utilizing the latest technology. Then he added cost controls. The man was very smart. He came in and laid the foundation, got the basics solid. When the basics are solid, a company can feel secure enough to experiment. Now Jack is working to create what he calls the boundaryless organization—a company where there is a free and integrated exchange of ideas, inspiration, and resources; where the energy moves to where the action is.

ROSABETH KANTER: There's a famous Jack Welch story. One of his first moves when he came in as CEO was to set up sixty-five independent ventures, and he announced: "I don't care if all of them fail. I want people to learn to be entrepreneurs." He assigned some of his best people to these projects. That sent an unmistakable signal that he would put resources behind risk. Too many companies keep their best people working on the established winners. And, of course, failure becomes a self-fulfilling prophecy when only lesser talent is assigned to a project.

FRED WIERSEMA: It's amazing how many failures companies and individuals can endure and still retain their optimism and enthusiasm. Even with the very best talent working on a project, nine times out of ten it won't yield a winner.

JOHN KAO: Companies need resilient people who can tolerate the inevitable ups and downs. Hiring these kinds of people should be a primary focus for any company seeking to bolster its level of innovation. That said, I don't think there's one right way to retool hiring and recruitment. Pfizer likes to hire PhDs right out of college and then train them in the Pfizer way of doing things. Likewise, at 3M people are promoted from the inside. Other companies like to recruit outsiders, people with terrific track records of innovation. They like the injection of fresh blood, fresh perspective.

FRED WIERSEMA: I don't think *any* company should hire people who aren't self-starting, who need regular deadlines and constant hand-holding. You want people who embrace uncertainty, take initiative, and aren't afraid of projects that have no immediately discernible direction.

Microsoft is a master at hiring talented, innovative people. Like so many pathbreaking companies, they have turned a process itself—in this case, hiring—into an innovation opportunity. The heart of the process is a series of unstructured, almost improvisational interviews. The usual suspects from HR don't conduct these interviews; people from throughout the company participate. And they're expected to ask meaningful and original questions, so they have to really invest in the procedure. Often one of the interviewers will have just come from a meeting in which people were grappling with a specific challenge and ask the prospective hire, "Now, how would you deal with that?" The comfort level with that kind of question reveals an awful lot about a person's ability to think on her feet and thrive in an unstructured environment.

JOHN KAO: You want people with a range of psychological profiles to interview the same candidate. This allows you to evaluate him from varying perspectives. Otherwise an interview becomes an instrument that screens out as much as it screens in. A traditional HR attitude is, "Oh, this person is great—he fits right in, he understands our culture. We feel really comfortable with him." Those, of course, can all be kisses of death when it comes to trying to bring in fresh perspective. How about hiring someone you feel a little bit *un*comfortable with? Friction creates sparks.

ROSABETH KANTER: These kinds of multiple interviews have another benefit. They send a signal that the company has a strong culture where people work across boundaries, where ideas are cross-fertilized.

FRED WIERSEMA: A very simple question can be very revealing; for example, "What are your work habits?" One person will answer, "I plunge in. It's really different every day. But I'll tell you, some days I go into a frenzy and get a hell of a lot done." Another person will say, "Well, I get to work at 8:30 every morning. I sit at my desk with a cup of coffee and a banana and check my e-mail. Then, beginning at 9:15 exactly, I work for three hours." If you're looking for a creative person who can roll with the punches, those two answers tell you everything you need to know.

A second question might be "What turns you on?" The answer you *don't* want to hear: "I finished my last project on time and within its budget." The answer that should be music to your ears: "Working with my team. Last month Kimberly had this crazy idea for a process improvement. It was so off the wall, we didn't even tell anyone. We just went to work on a small-scale prototype. Then, when we thought we had it all together, it turned out we'd made a big miscalculation and we had to go back to square one. Long story short—the whole thing came together. It works. Saves time and money. It was such a charge pulling that off." Yes!

ROSABETH KANTER: It isn't only the questions you ask the candidate. You want to listen very carefully to the questions the candidate asks *you*. Curiosity is the foundation, the soul of innovation. You want people who are voracious for information, and not just about their potential bailiwick but about the whole company. Look for how they accept and absorb information. Do they pose follow-up questions? Do they challenge a piece of information? Terrific!

FRED WIERSEMA: The hiring process is always anxiety-provoking for an applicant. Some very talented people are lousy at interviews. You have to take that into consideration. At Microsoft the uneasy person might not get hired, simply because they weren't aggressive or agile enough. But overall, you can read between the lines. You've got to size up a person's talent, not in interviewing but in terms of the job that you have in mind for her.

However, the process isn't a one-way street. The interviewer has a major challenge: to attract the talent. You have to remember that the best and brightest people are very much in demand. When they go in for an interview, they're auditioning the company as much as vice versa.

JOHN KAO: Of course, innovating your hiring process and then putting people into a stagnant company defeats the purpose. Innovation must be systematic.

In my seminars I always ask: "How many of you think innovation and creativity are strategically and fundamentally important for your business?" Between 90 and 98 percent of the audience raises its hands. My follow-up question is: "How many of you have an innovation system in place that your people understand and that leads to the realization of value on a reasonably consistent basis?" The hands drop to about 2 or 3 percent.

ROSABETH KANTER: Many companies have what they consider an innovation system. The problem is that most of them don't work very well. Often the systems consist primarily of screening ideas and denying resources to the majority of them. What's missing is encouragement, nurturing, and involvement.

I've diagrammed what I call the innovation pyramid. The goal is to have innovation going on at three different levels. At the top of the pyramid are a few big projects you're pretty sure will pay off. You can't have too many of them, because they require big investments. That's where the major focus is. In the middle of the pyramid is a portfolio of prototypes—experiments that are being developed. Think of this as your venture capital portfolio. Maybe 20 or 30 percent of these are going to bear fruit. At the base of the pyramid are an infinite number of incremental innovations taking place throughout the company. These can be small-scale personal experiments; they can be outside ideas appropriated by a sharp-eyed employee.

If you do it right, influence flows two ways in the pyramid. Those strategic bets at the top flow down to guide your portfolio of experiments and to communicate to every employee the direction the company is going. But influence also flows up. Sometimes it is the 3M style tinkering at the bottom of the pyramid that leads to cost-cutting process redesign and even highly profitable products. Depending on your company's specifics, you tailor how much you invest at the three levels.

Hopefully, this pyramid model helps a company understand where ideas come from and how they get reviewed and funded. And also how to guide them around roadblocks, and support and nurture them when they falter. Ideas are vulnerable. It takes time, effort, and care to make them real and then link them back to the rest of the organization. You know, the sales force doesn't always like new products. They mean a lot of extra work, and the incentive structure may not reward them for that work. You have to make sure that the whole organization is going to be receptive. You have to integrate the project into the mainstream of the company. Too often, sensational ideas are left hanging on the fringes. Then you risk somebody else coming along and scoring in the marketplace with what was originally your idea. That happens to a lot of companies.

You'll get your idea to market faster if you assemble representatives of all the constituent groups into a big team from the beginning. It doesn't mean they all have to be intimately involved in every step. But if they're all involved in planning, they can anticipate what changes have to be made in their own functions to be ready to receive the product.

JOHN KAO: If talented people see their ideas die because of mismanagement, they lose faith in the whole process of innovation. If your pyramid is out of balance, you wind up angering, alienating, and disappointing a lot of people.

ROSABETH KANTER: There are many reasons why companies lack innovation. Failure of the human imagination is not one of them. The failure is in the culture and the structure.

JOHN KAO: Ideas are the easy part.

ROSABETH KANTER: Exactly. The first thing companies say to me is: "We want more innovation." The second thing is: "Who else is doing it?"

FRED WIERSEMA: Nobody wants to be the first on the block. There's still an ingrained fear of risk in too many companies.

ROSABETH KANTER: There's a deadening tendency to name an innovation czar. It sends the wrong message. Innovation has to permeate an organization, be owned by *everyone*. Create a czar and people look to that person for guidance. Wrong. You want people to take initiative on their own.

JOHN KAO: True, but the commitment has to start at the top. It's no accident that the five companies in this book are, to a greater or lesser extent, built around a very influential and opinionated leader. They changed structures and priorities, set agendas, attracted talent, and reconfigured the game board so that everyone could play.

ROSABETH KANTER: I like the game board metaphor. CEOs control the environment—the design of the game and who gets to play. Also, a company's language has to be rewritten. Words have tremendous power and they should reflect a commitment to innovation.

JOHN KAO: I'm always impressed by the language innovative companies use. It's very sophisticated in its understanding of human behavior. They may not call it psychological, although that's clearly implicit. Pepsi-Cola has developed a statement that describes in human terms what it means to manage in an innovative environment. It provides a set of touchstones for managers.

ROSABETH KANTER: Of course, words must be backed up by action. Nothing is more dangerous than a conflict between a company's stated mission and the way it is actually run. That breeds rampant cynicism. One of the great innovation-killers is the admonition "You must deliver on your promises." What happens? To avoid failure, people promise only the most limited goals. You want to create a challenging atmosphere that embraces honest failures.

JOHN KAO: One of the keys is connecting people with each other and with the necessary resources. Perception is also important: Do people feel nurtured and supported? The CEO's job is akin to that of a studio head in the movie business. He might not actually do the creative work, but without his efforts to provide resources and context, exciting, innovative products just won't get produced.

ROSABETH KANTER: The CEO has to love the product, infuse it with excitement and glamour. The last thing you want is a number cruncher.

FRED WIERSEMA: Absolutely. Look at a guy like Al Dunlap, who clearly has no idea what innovation is all about. Dunlap comes in, slashes the product line, slashes development, and in doing so, basically squelches innovation. You might get a short-term fix, but over time you're going to pay. The exciting products won't be in the pipeline and morale will be in the gutter. It's antithetical to innovation.

ROSABETH KANTER: The Al Dunlaps of the world may create companies that are good at cutting costs and increasing efficiency, but ideas shut down. Cynicism sets in. People like Dunlap create moral, ideological vacuums. They're bad news for the future of American business.

JOHN KAO: Dunlap is a throwback to the myth of the general manager. There was a popular theory two or three decades ago that if you went to Harvard Business School, you could manage any company, whether it made razor blades, movies, or missiles. In fact, there are conglomerates that probably still believe in that myth. But that style of management negates the role of passion—the sine qua non of innovation. You have to make room for the irrational.

ROSABETH KANTER: Now you're touching on what I think is a popular misconception about innovation, one we were addressing with the pyramid model. Innovation is more than a brainstorm from above. Yes, creativity is essential. But managerial creativity is as important as product creativity. You need follow-through.

JOHN KAO: It's true—American companies need more creativity *everywhere* in their organizations. A lot of people have read business books that espouse a whack on the side of the head, a kick in the seat of the pants, lateral thinking stuff. Which is absolutely crucial. But it's just the first step.

ROSABETH KANTER: Innovation is the process of bringing new ideas into productive use. And, incidentally, the idea doesn't necessarily have to originate with you. Innovation is not necessarily invention. If you're the one who gets an idea into the marketplace, the payoff can be tremendous. The secret is building that bridge between the idea and its commercial viability. It's infinitely practical.

FRED WIERSEMA: It certainly should be. Innovation is *commercial* imagination.

ROSABETH KANTER: The danger is that this hot concept of lateral thinking will get blown out of proportion. I expect to see lots of business books with the word *intuition* in their titles. Then we'll have the predictable and unfortunate backlash when wild-eyed ideas will be deemphasized. Which is a pity, because they're critical. But they're hardly the whole ballgame. Every company needs a strategy, an innovation system, and quality production processes. Those are the foundations of success.

FRED WIERSEMA: There's a delicate balance between a company's more immediate economic needs and its long-term strategy. The danger is that a company will become so concerned about the marketplace that projects will be killed prematurely. In today's chaotic, technology-driven global economy, new applications are being discovered daily. What looks like a loser today could well be a winner tomorrow.

And vice versa. It takes real savvy and a lot of detailed knowledge to make the right decision on a project's future. A large part of the equation is the people who have invested their hearts and minds in the work. How do you keep them committed and energized when they know that months and years of effort could be for naught?

JOHN KAO: Projects are cut all the time. It brings up a key managerial paradox—you are both creator and destroyer. The manager is the person to whom creative people go for funding and support and trust, and he's also the one who pulls the plug. That's why empathy and intuition are so crucial. You have to make sure people understand all the reasons why a project is being killed. You also have to assure them that their work hasn't been in vain—that it has become part of the organization's knowledge bank and may prove to be a crucial catalyst for future innovation.

ROSABETH KANTER: IDEO, the San Francisco–based design company, is a master at documenting what it has learned on aborted projects. This knowledge is then made readily accessible on the company network. Incidentally, some very promising projects are just wrong for a company because they don't play to its strengths. You can't move in a hundred different directions simultaneously—you'll spread yourself too thin. This is where the strategic dimension comes in. Focus.

FRED WIERSEMA: The whole arena of knowledge-capturing and access is undergoing a profound technology-driven change.

ROSABETH KANTER: Suddenly the whole world is at your fingertips. DuPont, which traditionally hired scientists who worked exclusively in their own domains, has begun emphasizing internal and external communication networks.

JOHN KAO: These days the key creative community is an invisible college unto itself. The first global university. In the field of protease inhibitors, for example, there are probably less than a thousand world-class experts. They form a virtual network that stays in touch continuously. At Pfizer, DuPont, and Merck, specialists hang out—virtually, if not physically—with their colleagues around the globe. It has very little to do with corporate titles, so an organization has to be flexible. On one hand, you've got to own some talent, but on the other hand you've got to understand and access the networks outside your boundaries. Otherwise, you're just limiting yourself.

ROSABETH KANTER: The guiding principle should be: What feeds innovation? Novadisc, the pharmaceutical giant created by the recent merger of Sandoz and Ciba-Geigy, has set up a venture fund to provide entrepreneurial capital to people who are going to be displaced. If someone seizes on the merger as a chance to work independently, they want to help. Novadisc will then have the inside track on anything these nascent entrepreneurs come up with.

FRED WIERSEMA: Companies with fast product cycles face very different challenges. Rubbermaid manages to make dish drainers and trash cans exciting. The design is superb—a lot of their products are quite beautiful and actually sensual.

ROSABETH KANTER: Rubbermaid understands the thrill of discovery and has turned the work into fun. Everyone who works there knows that what they're doing makes life easier for millions of people every day. There was a classic article on organizational behavior in *Industrial Sociology*. The article analyzed assembly-line workers who had incredibly boring jobs but were incredibly productive. Their secret? They made the job into a game and created their own excitement. Every day was a challenge. And management made sure they were appreciated. Rubbermaid uses these same techniques.

Innovative companies create a great deal of internal competition. Not in a hostile sense, but positive, friendly competition that leads to pride of accomplishment. Rubbermaid has made workers very cognizant of the connection between what they do and their millions of customers.

JOHN KAO: There's a great story about Rubbermaid's Wolf Schmitt being in Paris with a few hours to kill. On the spur of the moment he went to the Louvre in search of inspiration for new product ideas.

ROSABETH KANTER: I call a serendipitous expedition like that "a far afield trip."

FRED WIERSEMA: Rubbermaid has the advantage of almost instant gratification. Compare that with the pharmaceutical industry. What could be more boring than a protracted development process and the knowledge that the odds of your work ever seeing the light of day are 100-to-1?

ROSABETH KANTER: Rubbermaid also engages people internally—everybody in the company uses the products. A food company I'm working with finally realized that "Hey, all of our employees eat. Maybe we should ask for their opinions and ideas." When you make everyday products, it's often easier to build a culture where people feel responsible for quality. Gillette, a terrific innovator, is an example. At its South Boston headquarters, anyone can volunteer to try the product, to come in and shave in the lab. They have managed to create glamour and sex appeal around an essentially mundane product. In fact, most people dread shaving. Xerox is another company where employee/users have tremendous input.

Decades of research have proven that the best innovation is user-driven. Many entrepreneurs are motivated by frustration with a current product and a belief they could build a better one. They want to be able to use their own product. In the ideal innovative culture there is a real harmony of interests between customer, employee, and leadership.

JOHN KAO: One of the most exciting companies I've observed over the last couple of years is Senco, a privately held company outside of Cincinnati that makes nail guns and industrial fasteners. You couldn't imagine anything more mundane. But the environment crackles with energy. They spend over 10 percent of revenue on knowledge-development, with a real emphasis on field trips and expeditions.

Key executives Brad Hoyt and Bill Hess set out to create a company infused with a sustainable entrepreneurial spirit. They're obsessive about keeping up with anything and everything—from changes in demographics to cultural trends—that affects the housing industry and worldwide house construction. They hire strategy companies to help them develop future scenarios. Nail gun technology has proven to be applicable to surgical fasteners, and the company has diversified in that direction. This is a company that is voracious about innovation.

ROSABETH KANTER: That's fascinating. Not only are they encouraging product and process innovation, but they're also creating the future. Giving employees a broad view of the world makes the work intellectually stimulating, and it's also a trigger for still more innovation. External stimulation can jar your thinking, spark inspiration, lead to new directions, add another perspective.

JOHN KAO: That's where the field trip comes in. It's play. Go to places—physical, emotional, and intellectual—where you've never been before. We have to think of ourselves as anthropologists, Margaret Meads of the business world. It could be as simple as surfing the Web for random information. I know a company that hired a teenager to travel around the world and photograph whatever he found interesting. The CEO of a *Fortune* 50 company used a hidden camera to film a store where his products were sold. He edited the footage into a video that he used to illustrate how people responded to the products.

FRED WIERSEMA: Videotape can be a fantastic innovation tool—it allows us to see the product through the customers' eyes.

ROSABETH KANTER: The more you can tighten that feedback loop between user and company, the better off you are. A software company I wrote about in *World Class* holds review sessions every week where they tear apart all the questions that have come in from customers. Not only do they have to answer the questions and solve the problems, but the information goes right to the product-development people. It's a very tight and accurate loop because it's done on a weekly basis.

JOHN KAO: In order to hear what its customers are trying to say, a company has to learn humility. For many companies that's extremely difficult.

FRED WIERSEMA: Arrogance is a major enemy of innovation. It precludes a willingness to learn.

ROSABETH KANTER: Most large companies have an enormous disconnect between R&D and the people who have direct customer contact. If you close those gaps, you can change the way a company thinks. Put some marketing people on the product-development team. And vice versa. You have to get people out of the bowels of the company and into the world.

Too often we see big companies trumpeting their desire for an infusion of new spirit and cutting-edge knowledge. They go out and buy small, innovative companies on that basis. Then the minute they take over, they ignore anything anybody in the acquired company has to say.

FRED WIERSEMA: They just aren't structured to absorb new information. These companies are their own worst enemy—and often they don't even realize it.

JOHN KAO: More businesspeople should strive for what the Zen Buddhists call "beginner's mind." It's a state free from preconceptions.

ROSABETH KANTER: The world is changing with unprecedented speed, so many of our preconceptions are obsolete. My seventeen-year-old son has had a flourishing consulting business for several years: He teaches senior executives how to use their personal computers. Al Gore was on target when he said, "You want to learn about the information superhighway? Find a twelve-year-old." Generally, twelve-year-olds don't have a lot of credibility in the business world. Maybe they should.

Some companies have been humbled by experience. They've coasted on a few successful products and desperately need follow-up winners. Or they were good at buying small companies with a promising product and then building them up. They haven't learned how to create exciting products themselves. The result: newfound humility and a willingness to at least listen to outside voices.

FRED WIERSEMA: That's when they bring in the consultants to shake up the status quo.

JOHN KAO: There's a big difference between shaking up the status quo and changing it. I care a lot more about creating something that's sustainable than about a quick shot in the arm. A legacy, not a lightning bolt. There's a misconception, a surprisingly frequent one at the highest levels, that innovation is a quick fix. We have money left in the budget, so let's get an innovation specialist to come in and jazz us up a little bit—as opposed to realizing that it's something that gets practiced 365 days a year or not at all.

ROSABETH KANTER: One company called me because they were losing market share. They had been through program after program, including a disastrous stab at reengineering. There was a tremendous backlash. And to his credit, the CEO announced: "This is not another program. This is the way we have to operate. I want everybody to have specific innovation goals in terms of product development. But let's also examine every aspect of how we do things to make sure that we're supporting those goals across the organization. Innovation is not the next fad; it's something that ought to be built into our business system."

JOHN KAO: Some of these companies make me think of heavy meat and butter eaters. They love their steaks and sauces, and the last thing they want to hear is that they're headed for heart disease. Then they have a heart attack, and suddenly they're willing to listen. Even then their motivation is short- to medium-term. In the back of their minds, you know they're dreaming of going back to that sirloin.

The most interesting companies are the ones that come out of the woodwork and say: "We want to harness the fundamental engine of growth. We're a $3 billion company and we want to be a $7 billion company. We want to step back and take a good hard look at what we can become." It's less like cardiac rehab and more like spring training.

If there isn't *serious* support at the senior level for comprehensive change, it just won't take. If I get a call from an executive who tells me the company is in a slump and wants me to come in and provide a little jolt of creativity, well, I know it's not going to fly. I can tell there's no buy-in from senior management.

FRED WIERSEMA: The biggest frustration for a consultant is being treated like a passing fancy. Today everyone is going to innovation retreats. The implication is that in two or three days people will learn to be creative. That's not the way life, or business, works. It takes continuous, sustained commitment to make a difference. As an outsider, there's only a certain amount you can accomplish. You encourage people to start changing and hope that over time it will catch on. Sometimes it does.

ROSABETH KANTER: I think retreats can be very valuable. To borrow a Tom Peters word, they can be liberating. You want individuals to tap into their own power and realize that taking action actually does have an impact. Some consultants argue that you need the whole system in place. I disagree.

FRED WIERSEMA: Sometimes profound change happens very quickly, and it's tremendously gratifying to see. After a three-day workshop, I've seen people dramatically improve the way they relate to their colleagues and customers. But in terms of company-wide innovation, a retreat can only scratch the surface.

JOHN KAO: I think we all agree that retreats are like a fast food meal—order me out a pizza with pepperoni and innovation with extra cheese.

ROSABETH KANTER: If a consultant is working on one function—a new training program or compensation system, for example—then there can be frustration at the rest of the organization. It's as if you're using computers and they're still typing away on a Selectric. Today, no function is an island.

The first essential, to borrow from Socrates, is to know thyself. Companies should start with a brutally honest self-assessment. Systematically scrutinize every function and ask: "Do our practices in this area encourage or discourage innovation?" Once you finish this inventory, you can compare yourself to companies that are successful innovators. That doesn't mean you should rush out and copy them, but you can certainly avail yourself of tools that work for them—refitted to the specifics of your company, of course.

Your rewards and recognition practices are crucial aspects of this self-examination. Most companies discover that they're underrecognizing achievements in innovation. When I research a company, I like to read several years of employee newsletters—undertake an informal study of what it takes to get mentioned. Often, basically you get your name in for years of service. For doing time. But in highly innovative companies, the newsletters are full of examples of best practices, of heroes, of people and teams who have come up with good ideas. A very simple, immediate step a company can take is to set up some awards. Search for innovation heroes and make sure they're recognized. This allows you to take advantage of the innovators you've already got, to use them as role models.

JOHN KAO: These days, talent is very mobile. Companies that want to hold onto innovators had better be prepared to bestow more than a pat on the head. Cut them in economically. Otherwise they'll pack their bags and take their talents elsewhere.

The basic issue is how to engender the entrepreneurial spirit, the commercial imagination. Money works. Period. However, there's a major caveat here. Creating wealth for some people and not for others can lead to resentment and division. It's something that has to be addressed.

ROSABETH KANTER: There are places where innovators don't even get a pat on the head. But John is absolutely right. More important than a mention in a newsletter is having people share in the economic value they have helped to create.

FRED WIERSEMA: And it's good for the company. Kingston Technology, the world's largest independent maker of computer memory boards, recently divided $100 million among its 523 employees. The company, based in southern

California, is one of the world's leading innovators. Since its founding in a garage in 1987, the company has had a hard-and-fast rule that employees get 10 percent of the profits. When the company was recently sold to the Softbank Corporation, a Japanese conglomerate, for a billion dollars, the employees' share came to $100 million. As co-founder John Tu said, "What makes or breaks a company is not one or two people, it's a team. So you have to share. They work just as hard as you do, probably harder. It's simple. It's common sense." The company also gives quarterly bonuses and an average of $300 to every employee at Thanksgiving. Job descriptions are blurred, and people are free to move between projects and take personal initiative. There is no executive dining room, no reserved parking places, and the founders sit in low-walled cubicles like everyone else. There is a tradition of helping one another in times of personal crisis, lunch is free on Friday, and there are free tampons in the women's restrooms. And the payoff for all this innovation has been astonishing growth and record profits. Treating people well is good business. Period.

On a larger scale, Microsoft is famous for spreading the wealth around. It also makes sure everyone knows who the innovators are. This creates a feeding frenzy, because everybody wants to get the best people on their team.

JOHN KAO: It's a little bit like creating an internal free market for ideas and resources. Talented people are free to migrate to interesting projects. This kind of shape-shifting can only happen if the typical restricting environment is deconstructed.

FRED WIERSEMA: At DuPont you sell new ideas by building internal support and then going to leadership to fight for resources. Competition between teams and units for resources is healthy.

ROSABETH KANTER: At General Electric Medical Systems, people with good ideas know management will listen to them. If they like what they hear, they'll authorize unallocated funds immediately. Nobody has to wait until the next budget cycle to get moving.

JOHN KAO: Oticon, a Danish company that makes hearing aids, has completely deconstructed itself. In one fell swoop they abolished job descriptions, functional specialization, resource-allocation systems, reporting relationships, and geographically based offices. The company basically became a roster of projects.

ROSABETH KANTER: That's how Gore-Tex does it. No titles. Tons of projects.

JOHN KAO: This represents a fundamental shift in the way managers need to view their role. It's not necessarily about managing people so that their behavior conforms with your model of what you want them to do. In this new paradigm the manager becomes an enabler as opposed to a controller.

The computer revolution plays a huge role in this restructuring. There is a virtual space that links resources, people, and projects. It's more democratic, less hierarchical, and more efficient. You can simply put it out there for everyone to see. Oticon basically puts all of its projects on-line. People decide for themselves which projects best suit their interests and what they want to learn—and, of course, their skills.

ROSABETH KANTER: Topic-specific networks are a superb tool. DuPont has over four hundred official networks worldwide that focus on a particular technology, process, or interest. They are in continual communication on-line. These networks solve problems, but they also provide a vehicle for people to test ideas and stimulate their intellects.

The concept of idea scouts is gaining in popularity. Canon and other highly innovative Japanese companies have made the search for new ideas a formal part of people's jobs. In this country, the juice company Ocean Spray credits its phenomenal growth to its idea forum. *Everyone* in the company is encouraged to contribute. This led to the introduction of CranApple, one of the first blended juices. Again thanks to an idea scout, Ocean Spray was the first American company to use paper bottles, which helped them take market share from Coca-Cola and Minute Maid.

JOHN KAO: Hundreds of companies do scenario planning, which is basically imagining what tomorrow will look like.

Shell was one of the pioneers in the technique. Instead of thinking about the future just in terms of oil prices, they would get together and ask: "OK, what are three or four alternative futures? How do we have to prepare for those futures? What is it that we have to do that's common to all of them?" That's innovative strategy. Some companies use actors who improvise possible scenarios about products, consumer behavior, and industry dynamics. Bear in mind that a lot of innovative ideas start with hunches about the future. There's a company in San Francisco called The Global Business Network that specializes in scenario planning. It has eighty clients.

FRED WIERSEMA: I like to have managers sit down with a blank piece of paper and imagine that they had the opportunity to build their company from scratch. How would it be structured? How would it be innovative? Who would the people be? What would the technology look like? When they're done creating their dream company, we compare it to where they are right now.

This exercise always leads to a stimulating discussion, a tremendous rush of ideas, and a renewed sense of possibility. This is invariably followed by a letdown as the daunting nature of the task sets in. People realize how far they are from where they want to be.

ROSABETH KANTER: It all comes back to unleashing the imagination. I'm always amazed at the remarkable innovations companies come up with. Powersoft actually has nonemployee volunteers who work the company's on-line networks. The program is called Team Powersoft—thirty professionals who, for two hours every day, answer customer questions about the company's products. What's in it for the volunteers? They get early access to the products. They get professional stature because you have to be screened to get on the team. They get access to the brightest minds in the field. And they get public acknowledgment because other users know them as experts. Three times a year the company pays travel expenses for the volunteers to come together as a group. For the $150,000 a year it costs to support this, the company gets millions of dollars worth of talent; brilliant unpaid "employees" who wouldn't take a customer service job in the first place. Microsoft has something similar, as does Boylan.

JOHN KAO: Tom Sawyer and the picket fence. Technology is fantastic at busting boundaries. You can build a community outside the organization.

ROSABETH KANTER: As an added benefit, the company gets impartial input on what people in the real world are saying about their products.

JOHN KAO: Powersoft is trying mightily to avoid the fate that befalls almost all successful companies—complacency.

ROSABETH KANTER: That's certainly been true historically. The classic definition of innovation was Joseph Schumpeter's: creative destruction. His theory was that innovation always comes from outside an industry's current leaders because they have too much at stake in exploiting what they've already got.

Really smart companies today are trying to avoid that fate. It begins by understanding the success-coast-fade cycle that products go through. I was very impressed by General Electric Medical Systems. The company's CAT-scan has 80 percent worldwide market share, but they're working hard to make it obsolete. Their own winner. That's not easy to do. The trick is to stick with your mavericks on these fronts— otherwise they'll get eaten up by the people who have a stake in milking the established line.

JOHN KAO: This is where leadership comes in.

FRED WIERSEMA: Ned Johnson at Fidelity is a perfect example. His message is: "OK, folks, put together a new venture even if it's going to cannibalize some of the old ones." Nothing is sacred. He'll have two teams going after the same opportunity. Ned is a master at fomenting healthy internal competition.

ROSABETH KANTER: I met one Fidelity employee who had five business cards because he was involved in five different projects.

We shouldn't minimize the difficulty of this self-cannibalization. A lot of CEOs and managers love what they do and love the products. They have to learn to let go. Sentiment can stymie innovation. You have to temper your love with understanding that as things grow, they change, and sometimes they die.

JOHN KAO: It isn't only managers who have trouble letting go. Creative people can become very attached to their babies. Managing talented people is an art in itself.

FRED WIERSEMA: I've dealt with a lot of creative, innovative people in my career. I know from my years in advertising that most copywriters fall into two categories. The first are the ones that come up with that breakthrough idea—the night before you have a major presentation. They can turn your hair gray and make for a lot of Maalox moments. The other kind of copywriter likes to work in a group, sitting around tossing out concepts, each person building on the others' ideas. These joint creativity sessions will yield a lot of terrific copy, but they're less likely to yield the earth-shattering concept that the lone genius will come up with.

JOHN KAO: The ideal is to balance the two creative types. The great managers I know would probably say that, by and large, the most interesting ideas come about through interaction. It's crucial to pose an interesting challenge. Leonardo da Vinci could probably stare at his navel and find intriguing challenges, but in business, most of them come about through interaction. By combining different points of view, you create a catalyst.

Companies that are smart about this understand that it's an architectural thing. You want to simulate a high degree of informal, unplanned discussion, but not at the expense of privacy. People must be able to go off by themselves when they need to. It's not an either-or proposition. The key is creating a structure that enables and encourages both dialogue and reflection. Cross-functional teams are an excellent mechanism to achieve this.

FRED WIERSEMA: Multidisciplinary teams are virtually ubiquitous these days. We all know the reasons: They spark creativity, provide additional insight and points of view, and increase exposure to the big picture. But I think they have a real potential to act as straitjackets to innovation. They tend to nip things in the bud, set boundaries. Creative folks in R&D should be able to let their imaginations run wild, with no censoring of ideas. That comes later, when the project has to fight for budget by proving its marketability. But a lot of ideas that eventually become winners start life looking patently absurd. Today, with someone from marketing on the team, you've got the voice of reason second-guessing your creators from day one. I'm not saying teams don't work. But I do think there's a potential for inhibiting creativity inherent in their structure.

JOHN KAO: It depends how they're managed.

FRED WIERSEMA: Yes. It's crucial to understand what you're trying to accomplish. If it's raw innovation, then the creators should be running things. If it's incremental improvements, then marketing should have a larger say. Again, it comes down to balance. Who runs these multidisciplinary teams is very important.

JOHN KAO: No one said innovation was easy.

ROSABETH KANTER: But it's imperative.

FRED WIERSEMA: New technologies are making Marshall McLuhan's prophecy about the global village a reality. The 21st century will bring unprecedented levels of opportunity—and competition, chaos, and change. Only those companies that learn to live and breathe *continuous* innovation will thrive in this exciting new world.

JOHN KAO: On that note, let's get some lunch.

ROSABETH KANTER: I know a terrific restaurant around the corner. The chef is wildly innovative. And the place is always packed.

3M (Minnesota Mining and Manufacturing Company)

"Vision is the engine that drives our enterprise."

DR. WILLIAM E. COYNE
SENIOR VICE PRESIDENT, RESEARCH AND DEVELOPMENT

If you asked me to describe 3M in one sentence, here's what I would say: "At 3M, we live by our wits."

Innovation may be an important element of other corporate strategies; but for us, at 3M, innovation essentially *is* our strategy.

Every year, we invest up to seven cents of every sales dollar—$883 million in 1995 alone—on research and development. We do this because we know that our future depends on maintaining a continuous flow of profitable new products to expand and update our existing base of fifty thousand products.

Our focus on innovation—and some of our tools of innovation—go back to the early days of Minnesota Mining and Manufacturing Company. For nine decades, 3M has been balancing on the innovation high wire, and we have prospered as a result. Our success is attributable to our ability to attract imaginative and productive people, create a challenging environment, design an organization that doesn't get in people's way, and offer rewards that nourish both self-esteem and personal bank accounts.

We synchronize all of this with our determination not only to keep up with the needs of our customers but also to anticipate those needs.

In our early days, we realized that in order to create products that truly solved customer problems we had to get our sales representatives and technical people past the purchasing office and onto factory floors where our products were being used.

This approach traces back to our first successes, which followed a decade of struggle and near failure. That disappointing decade began in 1902, when a group of five investors founded the company in Two Harbors, Minnesota, on the northwestern shore of Lake Superior.

The founders' intent was to mine corundum, an abrasive mineral used to make sandpaper. When the corundum deposit turned out to be nothing more than a low-grade look-alike, 3M began manufacturing sandpaper to survive.

Only after the company hired William L. McKnight, a young farm boy from South Dakota, as a $10.50-a-week bookkeeper, did we begin to emerge as a viable business. That was in 1910. Some years later, it was McKnight in his new role as a sales manager who instructed our sales representatives to go "behind the smokestacks," as he put it, to truly understand customers' problems.

That was how we discovered that curved or recessed surfaces presented real problems to automobile body shop workers. The contours were difficult to sand using conventional abrasives with their semirigid paper backing, and the dust from sanding was an irritant that caused chronic health problems. Acting on that intelligence, we developed 3M-Ite, a cloth abrasive that was more flexible than sandpaper, and Wet-or-Dry sandpaper, which could be used wet, keeping dust to a minimum.

The two products moved the company into the black and set us on the path we have followed ever since: We identify customer problems, anticipate their unarticulated needs, and come up with innovative solutions. We are *not* a commodity marketer. We could not survive on me-too products or product extensions. Granted, a lot of risk is involved in emphasizing the new and untried; but it's far riskier to rely on the comfortable and familiar. Putting bells and whistles on the buggy didn't distract consumer attention from the horseless carriage, and no combination of better keyboards and correction ribbons could save the typewriter when computers and word-processing software appeared on the scene.

In our case, the risks associated with introducing the new and untried are minimized by the diversity of our fifty thousand products. We are involved in so many businesses and markets that a problem in one has a minimal effect on our overall business.

Echoing William McKnight's advice to his sales representatives, we urge our employees to be creative and exercise foresight. They all know that we expect them to find the products that will provide for our future by providing for our customers' futures. It's not up to the customers to ask for the products they need; it's our job to recognize the clues, unearth customers' unstated problems, anticipate their hidden needs, and devise the product-solutions.

Let me give you an example. The promotional graphics industry had a long-standing, but unexpressed, problem. Screen printing is a complex process that's fine for producing high-volume runs of the colorful advertising and informational displays that decorate buildings and the sides of trucks. Hand painting, however, was the only economically feasible way to create just a few signs, and hand painting simply does not match the consistency and quality of screen printing.

Responding to our sales reps' knowledge of the sign-graphics industry, our Commercial Graphics Division developed its Scotchprint Electronic Imaging System, which has redefined competition in the sign industry. Our Scotchprint system uses an imaging technology similar to that of a color copier to produce signs in low volume. The signs the system produces equal the quality and consistency of screen-printed signs at a cost that's economical for small-volume orders.

The second generation of this product, Scotchprint II, challenges the screen-printing industry even for high-volume applications. Our customers can now produce any number of graphic displays—starting from a minimum of one. Furthermore, they can easily adjust shape and size to fit each particular application. The screen-printing method requires one size and shape to fit all.

MICROREPLICATION INSIDE

As laptop computers proliferated in the marketplace, manufacturers struggled with power problems. They tried to juggle the conflicting demands of longer battery life for extended performance with the size and weight considerations of smaller batteries.

Our people came up with an answer that sidestepped the problem: They devised a solution that allowed for longer battery life *and* smaller size. We discovered that the problem wasn't battery power, it was screen brightness.

We found a way to make screens brighter with less power, using our microreplication technology; this technique changes the surface structure of materials, altering their performance characteristics. We used microreplication to produce a screen cover containing millions of microscopic but optically perfect lenses. As the top layer of a laptop-computer screen, the plastic film concentrates light and can produce a bright screen image using only one bulb instead of two. Naturally, the single bulb works fine with a smaller battery.

As we began to understand the emerging market for efficient, effective flat-panel displays, we identified an array of additional proprietary 3M technologies that could further improve the performance of laptop screens.

CASTING ABOUT FOR SOLUTIONS

Sometimes, serendipity points us in the right direction. That happened when William McKnight, by this time chairman and chief executive officer, broke his leg and was forced to wear the heavy, bulky plaster cast of that day. He wondered aloud whether our scientists could develop something "less barbaric"—and they did.

Until then, plaster casts had changed little since the 1700s, when cloth dipped in wet plaster displaced plaster alone for encasing broken limbs. 3M acquired a technology for a synthetic material that was lighter and stronger than plaster but required cumbersome ultraviolet lighting equipment to harden the material. With 3M enhancements to that technology, we developed the first *successful* fiberglass-reinforced synthetic casting tape. That material—Scotchcast Casting Tape—hardens completely in a few minutes, while plaster casts can take up to a day to harden. Today, Scotchcast material is the standard orthopedic casting material.

THE 15 PERCENT SOLUTION

By now, you must be wondering just how 3M inspires company-wide eagerness to innovate. Part of the answer is that we've institutionalized innovation with our 15 percent rule, which allows all technical personnel to dedicate as much as 15 percent of their time to working on projects of their own choosing. They need no approvals. They don't even have to *tell* management about what they're working on.

It should come as no surprise that this rule also originated with William McKnight. During one of his visits to our labs, McKnight came upon Richard G. Drew. Although Drew was a professional banjo player, he was taking an engineering correspondence course, and that had helped him secure a position in quality control.

"What are you doing?" McKnight demanded when he saw the young man involved in something that clearly fell outside his responsibilities in quality control. Drew explained that during a visit to an auto body shop, he'd watched painters working on two-tone jobs and that the glue-and-paper approach they used for keeping neat lines between colors was anything but reliable. Since then, he continued, he'd been trying to make a crinkly backed tape that would be easier to remove from a newly painted car.

McKnight was far from impressed. He ordered Drew to abandon the project, insisting that it would never work. Ignoring that order, Drew went on to invent masking tape, one of 3M's breakthrough products. Drew's perseverance also put us on track for our defining product, Scotch tape. Today, 3M makes more than nine hundred varieties of Scotch tape for home, office, and factory.

As a result of Drew's success, McKnight decided there was great value in giving innovators creative license, recognizing that sometimes the best thing management can do is step aside and do nothing.

The juxtaposition of Drew's stubborn inventiveness and McKnight's enlightenment led to what we call the 15 percent rule. We encourage our technical employees to use 15 percent of their time pursuing their own ideas—without regard to assigned tasks.

Nobody meters or monitors our people's use of their

15 percent time. They know they have our support and encouragement to work on their own ideas. One scientist may use the time to visit another laboratory; a second might choose to visit customers. Often people use their time to help solve a problem that's occupying the attention of a colleague in another division.

Recently a researcher in our abrasives division used his time to explore a notion that had never occurred to anyone else. He wanted to investigate the applicability of our microreplication technology to sandpaper, so he studied the technology and experimented with it as an abrasive. The upshot was a metal-finishing product that has transformed the sandpaper industry. This microstructured abrasive works faster and imparts a better finish than conventional sandpaper. Because the new product is so much more efficient, it has established new standards for precision finishing.

CROSS-POLLINATION EQUALS INNOVATION

The microstructured abrasive was not the first product that emerged from the impulse to take a technology from one part of 3M's business and apply it elsewhere. In the 1960s, for example, we used an early version of our microreplication technology to produce a thin, lightweight, inexpensive plastic lens to replace the thick, heavy, expensive glass lenses in overhead projectors. The considerably improved image quality combined with a much more affordable price tag made overhead projectors a staple of classrooms and conference rooms.

In addition to its roles in computer screens, abrasives, and overhead projectors, microreplication technology has yielded material that makes reflective highway signs three times brighter than our previous best, a mechanical fastener for disposable diapers, and identification cards designed to put counterfeiters out of business. And you can bet that we have many other applications already in the works.

Such developments reflect a high level of networking among our technical people. We encourage—both formally and informally—interdepartmental conversation. Traditional organizations keep researchers and engineers within their own areas or divisions and expect loyalty to their own divisions. At 3M, we work hard to instill in our people a strong sense of attachment to the company as a whole. We want to sustain our tradition of technical people crossing departmental lines to help one another and share information about projects and technologies.

One way we have encouraged cooperation is by forming 3M's Technical Forum, an organization to which all our technical people belong. Forum programs range from lectures by Nobel Laureates to problem-solving sessions in which divisions present their most recent technical nightmares with the hopes that other colleagues will find answers for them. The forum also sponsors an annual event, at which each division puts up a booth to show off its latest technologies. It also sponsors specialty subgroups, called chapters. Each chapter deals with a scientific discipline, such as polymer chemistry or coating processes. Scientists in each discipline can gather to compare notes and share their technical experience and prowess. It helps to know that every 3M scientist outside of the discipline is only a telephone call away.

MANAGING FOR CREATIVITY

Management at 3M works continuously to refine its role, but the core of our mission has remained constant. Our goal is to communicate a single, enduring message throughout the company: Be creative and innovative. At the same time, we know that it is up to management to sustain a culture that encourages creation and innovation and enhances opportunities for success.

For example, we do not expect every—or even almost every—idea or project to pay off. As early as 1925, a 3M technical manual declared: "Every idea evolved should have a chance to prove its worth, and this is true for two reasons: 1) if it is good, we want it; 2) if it is not good, we will have purchased our insurance and peace of mind when we have proved it impractical."

When innovation is your goal, not only must you anticipate high risk, you must also regard failure as an opportunity to learn rather than an occasion for punishment. Our people know we understand that.

Managers at 3M do perform such traditional tasks as clarifying the company's goals and setting objectives. We let our people know what we want them to accomplish. But—and it is a very big *but*—we do *not* tell them how to achieve those goals. We think that by giving employees the freedom to find new paths to new solutions, we are unleashing their creativity.

Division management reflects the corporate attitude. Each of our forty-five divisions is oriented toward its specific customer base. And each is a business unto itself, with its own general manager, marketing director, technical director, human resources director, manufacturing director, and national sales manager. Divisional autonomy allows each unit to focus its energies directly on its customers' particular needs.

Its independence in no way compromises each individual division's access to the resources of the larger company. The divisions' technical directors are responsible for communicating their customers' needs to technologists throughout 3M. It's a 3M axiom that "products belong to the division, but technologies belong to the company."

For many decades, 3M has pursued a strategy of setting "stretch targets." It's based on the premise that ordinary goals inspire ordinary achievement. Prior to 1992, our target was to achieve 25 percent of annual sales from products that had been around for no more than five years. As tough as it was to hit that target, we managed to meet it pretty routinely.

In 1992, however, noting that product life cycles were shrinking and customer needs were changing faster than ever, L. D. DeSimone, our chairman and chief executive officer, raised the new-product imperative: 30 percent of all sales must come from products that had been around no longer than four years. That challenge really sparked the creative fires of the entire company, and within two years we were meeting the 30/4 goal. (We were at 27/4 in 1995, due to a reorganization in July 1995 in which our imaging and data-products businesses formed a new, independent company, Imation, Inc., and they took many new products with them.)

Our success came in part because of a renewed drive to create new products that would truly change the competitive rules in a market. One new product that emerged from that push was the Scotch-Brite Never Rust Scouring Pad. In only a few months—the fastest turnaround time in 3M's history—our people were able to introduce the pads—which we make out of recycled plastic soda bottles—to the commercial market. Scotch-Brite redefined a market that for seventy-five years had been, as we like to say, "asleep in the soap dish."

MOTIVATION: AWARDS AND REWARDS

The customary rewards and reinforcements for creativity and innovation are, of course, salary increases and promotions. In addition, 3M instituted the following programs and awards to let our people know that both management and their peers value their contributions.

• *Golden Step Award.* Every year, with considerable celebration, 3M recognizes teams whose new products have achieved $5 million in profitable sales within three years of hitting the market. In 1995, we recognized forty-three such teams.

• *Technical Circle of Excellence.* Based on the theory that coworkers are better positioned than their managers to assess one another's abilities and achievements, we ask the entire technical community to nominate those who excel either on their own or as mentors. In 1995, 255 people earned division-level honors and 18 earned corporate-level recognition.

• *Carlton Society.* We established this honorary organization in 1963 to recognize extraordinary contributions to 3M's science and technology. Its members include the inventors of Post-it Notes, Scotch Magic Transparent, and Scotchgard fabric protector. Richard P. Carlton, the engineer in whose honor we named the society, was 3M's first employee with a college-level technical degree.

• *Genesis Grants.* When technical people come up with ideas that do not fit into their division's business plan, they may apply for a corporate grant to pursue their ideas. In 1996, we awarded eleven such grants, ranging from $15,000 to $75,000.

• *Alpha Grants.* We award these grants for innovations in administrative, marketing, and other nontechnical areas.

3M, as I have already emphasized, places the highest value on innovation and new products. Our promotion policies reflect our supreme regard for such achievements. We reward not only good business managers but also people who help create new opportunities.

Consider the career of Lew Lehr, a technical service engineer in our tape division. When he discovered that hospitals used masking tape to tie up bundles of linens that were headed for the sterilizer, he suggested developing a special dye-coated tape that would change color once the linens had been sterilized. His idea led to autoclave tape, one of 3M's first health-care products.

Lehr also worked with surgeons at the Cleveland Clinic to develop adhesive-backed surgical drapes that would help reduce the risk of infection during operations. The surgeons thought the drape was terrific, but Lehr's manager believed the product would never take off. He instructed Lehr to cease and desist from all activities related to surgical drapes. "Yes, sir," Lehr agreed, but he failed to cancel his manufacturing instructions until after the factory had already turned out a whole year's supply. Using his spare time, he sold a government agency on the drapes, showed his boss the receipt, and convinced him to rescind the cease-and-desist order.

In the end, Lehr was promoted and eventually created a small medical-products division, which made such products as tapes to replace conventional sutures. It was, by the way, the very same Lew Lehr who suggested that 3M enter the pharmaceuticals business. And that was how I came to join 3M. The company hired me to create new molecules with pharmaceutical applications. Today, health-care business accounts for about 15 percent of 3M's sales. Lehr's consistently clear vision and creativity kept earning him recognition and promotions, and in 1985 he retired as chairman and chief executive officer.

I'm convinced that 3M will always be able to attract and keep people like Lew Lehr because we maintain such a strong focus on technology and innovation. I, myself, joined 3M because I knew that the company met its new-product goals and financial objectives by relying heavily on technical people—people like me. I figured that 3M must have been cultivating a nourishing atmosphere, and my assumption has proven correct since I arrived here—nearly thirty years ago.

Such longevity, incidentally, is not at all unusual at 3M. We attract and keep top-flight people because the company has a clear vision of what it should be; we communicate that vision effectively; and we make sure our people realize that management knows how precious they are to the company.

Our vision is simple: We want to be the most innovative company in the world. And we expect that our people will validate that vision in everything they do. That is the ultimate stretch target, continually changing to anticipate business and technology. Our vision is the engine that drives our enterprise.

COMPANY PROFILE

3M (MINNESOTA MINING AND MANUFACTURING COMPANY)

Business description	Diversified manufacturing
Founded	1902
Annual sales	$13.5 billion
Annual R&D expenditure	$.9 billion
R&D as a percent of sales	6.6%
Net income before taxes	$1.3 billion
Net income after taxes	$1 billion
Number of employees worldwide	70,687
Number of employees in R&D	6,500

PRIMARY 3M BRANDS

3M

Scotch

Post-it

Scotch-Brite

Scotchgard

O-Cel-O

SELECTED 3M PRODUCTS

Industrial and Consumer Sector

3M Structural Adhesives

3M Structured Abrasives

Confirm Security Laminates and Labels

Durel Electroluminescent Lighting

Filtrete Air Filter Media

Fluorel Fluorelastomers

Post-it Notes

Scotch Magic Transparent Tape

Scotch-Brite Abrasive Products

Scotch-Brite Scouring Pads

Scotchflex Cables and Connectors

Scotchlite Reflective Sheeting

Scotchlok Electrical Connectors

Scotchmate Hook-and-Loop Reclosable Fasteners

Scotchmount Double Coated Foam Tape

Scotchtint Sun Control Window Films

Thinsulate Insulation

Velostat Electrically Conductive Materials

VHB (Very High Bond) Acrylic Foam Tapes

Life Sciences Sector

3M Dental Electronic Anesthesia

3M Organic Vapor Respirator

Buf-Puf Cleansing Sponge

Concise Dental Restorative Materials

Ioban 2 Antimicrobial Skin Prepping System

Littman Stethoscope

Maxair Metered Dose Inhaler

Micropore Medical Tapes

Precise Medical Staplers and Supplies

Precise Mousing Surface for Computers

Sarns Membrane Oxygenator for Open Heart Surgery

Scotchcal Graphic Films

Scotchcast Orthopedic Casting Materials

Scotchlite Reflective Sheeting

Scotchprint Electronic Graphic System

Steri-Drape Surgical Drapes

Tambocor (flecainide acetate) Antiarrhythmic Agent

Tattle-Tape Security Strip

Tegaderm Medical Dressings

Transcend Ceramic Bracket System (braces)

Unitek Dental Crowns and Supplies

Traffic and Safety Products

Scotchlite Diamond Grade Reflective Sheeting for traffic signs

Brightness Enhancement Film

Security Laminates

Thinsulate Insulation

Commercial Graphics and Advertising Services

Scotchprint Electronic Graphic System

3M Floor Graphics

Our 1995 results were helped by a record flow of new products, by continued success in international markets, and by solid productivity gains.

During the year, we generated $855 million in first-year sales of new products, up 37 percent from 1994.

Twenty-seven percent of our 1996 sales came from products new within the past four years, compared with 26 percent in 1994.

. . . 3M's record of innovation and its reputation as a premier organization were validated again in 1995. We received the National Medal of Technology—the highest award bestowed by the President of the United States for technological achievement—for the many innovations and thousands of successful products 3M has introduced over nine decades.

L. D. DeSimone, Chairman of the Board and Chief Executive Officer
1995 Annual Report

Fact: 3M pioneered sandpaper, masking tape, transparent tape, repositionable notes, adhesive-backed surgical drapes, synthetic casting materials, and reflective sheeting for traffic safety. Among other 3M firsts are diaper tape, electrical tape, and maintenance-free respirators.

Fact: 3M has companies in sixty-one countries and sells its fifty thousand products in more than two hundred nations. 3M has manufacturing operations in more than forty countries and conducts research and development in twenty-five.

E. I. du Pont de Nemours and Company, Inc.

"Upset the natural equilibrium."

DR. JOSEPH MILLER
CHIEF TECHNOLOGY OFFICER AND SENIOR VICE PRESIDENT, RESEARCH AND DEVELOPMENT

First of all, it is important to understand the function of our research organization—one which we find unique to DuPont. To my mind, the primary responsibility of DuPont's research organization is to challenge the status quo. We must be committed to upsetting the natural equilibrium and pushing the company to consider the new strategic possibilities that our scientists' discoveries make possible. And we do that when we develop an entirely new process for making the raw materials for Lycra spandex fiber or when we open new markets by designing a device that measures bacteria in food.

It's up to us to make sure the company never decides to put the research function and its flow of new ideas on hold.

There are some companies that, after enjoying success for a while, forget that innovation is a critical component of continued success. DuPont is almost two hundred years old, and we have certainly seen ups and downs in our commitment to innovation. But those experiences are what taught us that persistence is the price we must pay for research success.

Back in 1926, when the company's growth began to level off, DuPont family members called for aggressive diversification into new businesses. Charles Stine, who was then the head of research, wrote to the company leaders:

> We are including in the central Chemical Department's budget for 1927 an item of $20,000 to cover what may be called, for want of a better name, pure science or fundamental research work. The volume of fundamental work is rapidly losing ground as compared with the volume of applied research. In other words, applied research is facing a shortage of its principal raw materials.

Stine fought for that $20,000, received it and additional funds, and spent the next few years protecting fundamental research. The company backed him, and it was rewarded with a string of breakthrough products that included nylon, neoprene, and moisture-proof cellophane—history-making products that fueled the creation of new polymer industries.

DuPont has continued to grow by applying new technology to both enhance current markets and create new markets. We have focused on sophisticated and demanding areas of chemistry. Better Things for Better Living—Through Chemistry, our slogan reads. Today's DuPont can boast:

• An environment that guides and focuses discovery research without stifling it

- A structured process that uses multidisciplinary teams to speed and guide our discoveries through the development of products or chemical processes

- Systems that assure that our technology development speaks to the needs of our customers

All that didn't evolve from a simple history, however. During DuPont's last seventy years, we experienced four separate bursts of technological innovation. Each began a cycle that lasted between fifteen and twenty years. And after each burst, the company experienced a period of consolidation, during which we were able to commercialize earlier discoveries, develop efficient manufacturing processes, and realize major cost reductions.

The fourth burst, for example, began in 1980, spurred in part by a major research audit, which identified factors that stimulate and hinder innovation. The audit included recommendations for improving the environment for innovation. A DuPont research director wrote at the time, "The real problem lies in a substantially reduced backlog of innovative new technology to form the growth industries of the '80s and '90s." The next decade's burst of innovation in life-sciences research laid the foundation for the DuPont–Merck Pharmaceutical Company.

DuPont invests more than $1 billion a year in research and development and employs more than three thousand engineers and scientists and two thousand technical support people.

Two-thirds of them work at our Experimental Station in Wilmington, Delaware, and the rest are scattered at company installations around the world, from Geneva to Yokohama.

At the Station, we conduct DuPont discovery research. This is the site of almost every one of our major discoveries. Its incredible record, spanning good years and bad, is a tribute to the company's willingness to support an endeavor that is inherently unpredictable and inevitably risky.

THE CARE AND FEEDING OF INNOVATION

Every year, we canvas our technical people to gauge how they feel about their work environment and the work itself. Year after year, I am impressed by the consistency of the survey results. Our people insist that it is their work rather than their environment that satisfies and motivates them. The challenges our scientists face and the opportunities available to them are remarkable motivators. They take great pleasure in their collaborations with colleagues and peers, inside and outside the company. Above all, they value their independence and the license to resist managers' efforts to redirect or otherwise control their work. Simply stated, we at DuPont reject the notion that it is possible to approach creation and innovation with a business school mentality. One of our corporate ads says it best: "There is nothing artificial about a moment of inspiration."

I work hard to make sure that our scientists have lots of those moments, but no research manager can teach people to be inspired. What I can do is sustain an atmosphere where exploration flourishes and people feel free to take chances and follow their intuition.

My responsibility reaches beyond that, however. Business management believes in the practical value of research and the necessity to take risks. Ultimately, I have to make sure that we deliver.

DuPont is determined to have research conform to our strengths and market needs, recognizing that some independence of choice is essential to sustain innovation. If we tie research too tightly to current business needs, our investigations will be driven only by short-term goals. On the other hand, our research must not be so long-term as to be irrelevant.

Like Charles Stine, I endeavor to lay out the strategic areas where research can most benefit the company: areas where the costs are reasonable and the risks acceptable. From that point we define targets. Our researchers are free to pursue their own goals as they will, with the understanding that we monitor their progress and, at various stages, will weigh the value of continuing their efforts.

IN THE BEGINNING. . .

At DuPont, almost everything starts with an idea in the laboratory. It takes about three thousand raw ideas to yield a dozen major projects, and from those we anticipate one successful entirely new product. Because it is so dear, an important discovery attracts company-wide attention. Everyone gets excited. People from the bench chemist to the chief executive officer want to get involved.

For research managers, the excitement is tempered by caution. They want their people at the bench to stay focused, and that often means keeping them free of interference from other company influences. Badly timed or misdirected attempts to take control can easily crush inspiration.

During the period that follows a research breakthrough, we analyze and exploit the idea for the opportunities it offers the company. At this point, we call on our research managers to perform another balancing act: They must relentlessly champion the idea throughout the organization, presenting it to those responsible for continuous/incremental improvements as well as to those who support discontinuous/radical breakthroughs. Radical innovation establishes and renews our competitive advantage; incremental improvements sustain it. Many companies, including DuPont, often pressure their leaders to focus on short-term incremental efforts alone. I remind our research managers that if the company is to thrive over time, we must resist that pressure.

I realize it isn't shocking to say that ultimately the whole innovation process comes down to risk management. When we make a discovery, we have only limited information and data. We operate on intuition. But as research progresses, we amass more information, and we explore the underlying assumptions one by one. Eventually, as we determine engineering needs and market potential, we can refine our assessment of the risk. That's when we can make intelligent decisions about whether or not to underwrite a discovery with more capital, people, and other resources.

I count myself lucky to have been involved in several such discovery projects. Each time, I emerge from the process convinced of an essential truth about industrial research. Even the most sophisticated project plans count for nothing if the project structure fails to give the technical people freedom to break away from the plan and follow their noses.

Not long after I joined the company as a young bench chemist, I had a most exhilarating laboratory experience. One of our researchers had just made a startling discovery. As graduate students we all had learned that when molecules of butadiene react chemically with other molecules, they invariably behave in a particular manner, according to certain "rules." To everyone's excitement, our researcher had found a catalyst that forced the molecules to react in exactly the opposite way, disobeying the so-called rules and creating a major opportunity for DuPont.

The company assembled a task force to explore the potential of that discovery, and I ended up on a research team that in the course of the next eighteen months grew from three people to more than a hundred. Every day was astonishing, as one discovery followed on the heels of another. Some were a result of serendipity, some of simple curiosity, and some of dogged hard work. With the new catalyst we could combine molecules in a new and unexpected way. For example, we synthesized adiponitrile, one of the intermediates that goes into nylon, for a much lower cost than ever before.

As we moved the project from small-scale development of adiponitrile toward full-scale production, the team kept pace, growing bigger and bigger. We began to envision a new plant, the way it would operate, the shape of the new reactor, and the recycling streams we would need. Within eight years, this "event" had progressed from a laboratory discovery to a new plant in Texas on the Sabine River, producing 100 million pounds of adiponitrile annually.

That was thirty years ago, and today we still do research that stems from that original discovery. We are poised to convert all DuPont's plants worldwide to using the third— even more cost-efficient—generation of that discovery technology. I remain confident that opportunities will continue to present themselves as long as we continue to look, and as long as we afford our researchers the freedom to explore.

THE MARKET CONNECTION

In the 1960s, the DuPont strategy called for pushing technology into the marketplace. During a period when the world was hungry for our new synthetic materials, that strategy proved to be a winner. But the world changes, and its demand for new materials has, to a great extent, been satisfied. Today, we are learning to listen to the marketplace rather than trying to dictate to it.

The history of products like Surlyn ionomer resins exemplifies that change. Richard Rees, a Welsh chemist, invented Surlyn during the 1960s. Never before had there been a plastic so tough, transparent, and shapable. Intuitively, we were certain that this new plastic held great market promise, but we could identify only one customer: an English manufacturer of ladies' shoes that used the material for scuff-proof heel tips.

Nevertheless, we proceeded to build a commercial plant for Surlyn while we waited for the new customers and applications to emerge. They did not. Our marketing people went into the field to search out potential customers. They demonstrated the remarkable characteristics of Surlyn, and they tailored the material to meet specific customer needs. Still, it was a tough sell. One of our market development veterans asserted, "We never sold a bag of Surlyn without blood on it."

Another of Surlyn's potentially valuable qualities was its remarkable resistance to abrasion. Company marketers believed that it would make a perfect coating for golf balls. But the major golf-ball manufacturers remained unimpressed. Their rubber-coated product's built-in obsolescence was a real plus, in their opinion. Our marketers, however, were not easily deterred. Finally, the director of research at a small golf-ball company agreed to go out with a DuPont salesperson on a summer morning while the grass was still dewy in the shade. The research director would give the DuPont product its ultimate test: If, when he hit the ball with a driver, the sound of the club on the ball made the right "click," he would opt for Surlyn. Fortunately for us, the click sounded good, and his company became the first to use Surlyn to coat its golf balls. Now, nearly every ball made in this country has a Surlyn coating, and *Golf Digest* magazine named Richard Rees—a man who never played golf—one of the top thirty-five contributors to the game.

Operating from a totally different perspective, large meatpackers resisted our marketers' suggestions that Surlyn would be useful in their business. They maintained that it cost too much, despite the fact that our researchers were able to demonstrate that Surlyn could actually save money by reducing spoilage because packages of Surlyn-wrapped meat could remain in cold rooms for six months without leaking.

Gradually, the versatile plastic found one new application after another. Today, bonded with foils, it wraps dog food, medications, and candy bars. It coats bumper guards, ski boots, and surfboards. By now you've probably guessed that Surlyn is the material that encloses those ubiquitous—and virtually impenetrable—blister packs. Remember, toughness and transparency.

The Surlyn saga taught us about market-driven development. Surlyn was a failure until we really addressed the market's needs. It turned out that the properties most of our customers initially came to value—click, adhesion, and oil resistance—did not match our preconceptions.

Large organizations are not generally good listeners. Too often they act as if what they have to tell is far more important than what the market has to teach them. Furthermore, it is often difficult for a big company to know when the right people are listening. We are working hard to make DuPont an exception.

Our customers too often face the challenge of finding the right listeners. Five years ago, for example, a DuPont customer was developing a new ink-jet printing system and had been meeting with our marketing people. The marketers understood that the customer's new system would require colored inks that met specifications far beyond the capabilities of available technologies. The inks needed to be stable under high shear, dry instantly, provide high-definition images, come in a wide range of brilliant colors, and hold up to moisture, abrasion, and ultraviolet radiation. Our customer's search for such inks had been fruitless and frustrating.

DuPont at the time viewed this customer narrowly, as one that purchased special electrostatic paper for engineering drawings. But when our paper product offering was rejected, the account manager took the opportunity to turn a no into a yes. He determined that what the customer really needed was printer ink of a higher quality, and he was certain that the appropriate technology existed somewhere in DuPont. With extreme persistence—and after a number of false starts—the account manager one day found himself talking to researchers in our automotive finishes—car paints—business.

Nowadays, it's not unusual to yank technical people from their labs for on-site research—or in this case, information gathering—so the account manager proceeded to arrange for the automotive-finishes researchers to meet with his customer. A brief discussion revealed that a technology the technical people had developed twelve years earlier might be the starting point for developing high-performance inks that could satisfy the customer's requirements. It was.

The marketing people in that case had identified a customer need, but they were not aware of the existing technology; the researchers were aware of the technology, but they were in no position to recognize the customer's need. Together the two constituencies defined a highly profitable new opportunity.

Clearly there is no standard prescription for such interplay between a company and its customers or between marketing people and researchers. Nevertheless, it is the necessary starting point for our innovation process and must be encouraged informally.

Let me give you another example of how we learn about our customers. When a customer calls to report that one of our products is not working properly, we respond instantly, dispatching technical representatives on the next train or plane. Too often, we find, our technical reps arrive only to find that the problem lies outside the realm of their particular expertise. In spite of our prompt response, the customer still has a problem.

Ever resourceful, several DuPont technical service representatives developed an alternative that has saved us and our customers considerable time and money. Under certain circumstances, we ask the customer to videotape the problem— at our expense—and send the tape to us for analysis. That way, if we need to send someone to the site, we can be sure it will be the right person. Soon, videoconferencing over the Internet will further enhance these efforts.

Here's another example. We continue to find new applications for Tyvek spunbonded products: It wraps letters (Tyvek is the material from which FedEx packs are made), houses under construction, and now automobiles. It was a two-person team—a market researcher and a product researcher—who discovered Tyvek's potential in the automobile market when they found a small car-cover manufacturer that became a key customer. Together our team designed the new product, and because DuPont had all the right people listening, the new car cover was a marketplace success.

Bringing new technology into the marketplace has always been a risky endeavor. Today, however, costs are higher than ever, while safety, environmental, and product liability risks grow increasingly complex. Under such conditions, we have learned not only to listen to customers but to collaborate with them. By combining marketing and technology skills, we all face lower risks.

NETWORKS AND COLLABORATIONS

In the modern world, knowledge—not labor, raw materials, or capital—is the key resource. Communications networks, the means by which we obtain and share knowledge, are therefore critical determinants of success or failure. Unless researchers network, they cannot create a product or bring it to market.

At DuPont, we consider networks essential tools of innovation, and we encourage them in every way—including financially.

DuPont supports more than four hundred formal and informal networks, most of which operate by means of fax, e-mail, electronic bulletin boards, or groupware. These networks transfer technologies throughout the company, reach decisions on preferred suppliers, develop standards and guidelines, conduct training and development workshops, help establish collaborations, and avoid duplication of effort. Consider these examples:

- *The Finite Element Analysis Center and Network.* Network members in Detroit, Geneva, and Wilmington produced a structural analysis of an automobile air intake manifold that led to the development of a manifold made of DuPont Zytel nylon.

- *The Corporate Maintenance Leadership Team* reduced maintenance costs by $200 million in one year.

- *The Process Sensor Network* transferred sensor technology throughout the company, making it possible for an individual plant to control its emissions and continue to operate.

- *The Adhesion Science and Practice Network.* Within a forty-eight-hour period, the network gathered data for a European customer on how to get a DuPont film to adhere to six different substrates.

What makes these networks work? At DuPont we hire primarily technical people: It's easier for technical people to learn about business than it is for business people to learn about technology. As a result, our people have a lot of mobility within the company, and newcomers often find themselves migrating through various positions within a business, from business to business, or from research in a business to research in a corporate lab. Along the way, people naturally build relationships that lead to networks of allies and mentors.

But not all the networks are spontaneous. A number of groups within the company, including our highest-ranking scientists, the DuPont Fellows, are always on the lookout for areas to which new networks could contribute. When we are working to form a new business, for example, we establish networks to tap the wide-ranging experience of new-business veterans.

We go to great lengths to ensure that everyone knows about existing networks, and we publicize their achievements. We pay for face-to-face meetings when other venues are inadequate. We provide groupware to facilitate the exchange of ideas within organizations and between business segments. Our Scientific Computing Division solves problems for groups all around the company. It has helped some thirty groups publicize their Intranet Web pages.

Beyond all that, our seamless e-mail system reaches the entire company, and more secure local area networks connect our research locations worldwide. We allow neither walls nor distance to obstruct communication.

Although two-thirds of our research networking today is electronic, face-to-face contacts are critical. There's no way to equal the synergy that develops when gifted people are in a room together, and that kind of communication is critical for our Experimental Station's four thousand people.

Many large companies put all their research personnel in the operating businesses; others have a central facility devoted solely to conducting long-range research. We believe our Experimental Station gives us a unique networking advantage because there we conduct both discovery and applied research. The people in discovery research have strong connections to the world of science, and they push the applied people to stay current. At the same time, the applied people maintain outstanding connections to the marketplace, and they push the fundamental people to take directions that are more relevant to market realities. Their interaction generates a tension that creates a competitive advantage.

Having so many of our technical people working together, we are able to sustain a sense of community that enhances innovation. Proximity is important. Scientists attend one another's research reviews. Their children go to school together and play on the same soccer and baseball fields. Every day as our scientists meet in the company cafeteria and chat about themselves and their work, instant networks are born.

At the Station, we've assembled a mix of people and skills that enables us to respond to challenges with confident effectiveness. When we wanted to develop a way to track sources of bacterial contamination in such microbe-prone products as pharmaceuticals, cosmetics, and food, we had no trouble assembling a collaborative group of microbiologists, molecular biologists, chemists, chemical engineers, electrical engineers, and software experts, all from within the Station. The group produced our Riboprinter Microbial Characterization system, a tabletop automated molecular-biology laboratory that can characterize and identify such harmful bacteria as *Salmonella* and *E. coli* in food as well as other substances. That single innovation is creating a quality management revolution in food processing and related industries. We've also formed a start-up subsidiary—Qualicon—to develop and market the technology.

The Station is a powerful symbol for the company as a whole, a concrete example of DuPont's preeminence in science and technology. Our reputation precedes us, so we can recruit topflight young scientists in America and abroad. Their enthusiasm and fresh points of view, unencumbered by preconceived notions, continually revitalize our excitement for the pursuit of new science.

THE POWER OF PARTNERSHIPS AND NETWORKING

For most of our history, we believed that we ourselves could handle all the necessary research. Now, DuPont's dedication to collaboration extends beyond the company itself, and that is something of a change. Our relationship with the university community, for example, once focused almost entirely on recruiting its graduates. But the world of science grows increasingly complex; we are no longer capable of doing everything ourselves, nor can we afford to. So we reach out.

Some of the partnerships we form are for the purpose only

of acquiring data for a specific project, but more often our goal is to sponsor research that will yield new ideas. We've made most of our alliances with organizations in North America and Western Europe, but we have also tapped expertise in India, Russia, and China. And a steady stream of visiting university professors and other scientists comes to work at the Station for short periods.

External networking makes the difference between success and failure when we've confronted overwhelming challenges. After the Montreal Protocol of 1987 called for the phasing out of all chlorofluorocarbons, DuPont was under the gun to find replacements for our Freon refrigerants. If we didn't manage to come up with solutions quickly, we would lose our hold on a major share of that market.

The technical demands were extraordinary. We needed a better understanding of the thermodynamic and transport properties of nonchlorine fluorocarbon mixtures, their material compatibility, lubricant solubility, toxity, and environmental effects. We needed better construction data for plant design, reactor design, and catalyst development. And we knew that on our own, we would be too slow.

Once we decided to go outside, we scoured the world for the right people. We worked with experts from abroad (Austria's Metallwerk Plansee GMBH and Germany's University of Hanover, for example) and with those closer to home (such as the University of Delaware, Georgia Tech, and the Department of the Navy). We connected with them all, and we networked with customers, too, asking them to help us test the performance of our new products in their compressors and with their lubricants.

The results? We were able to introduce five new families of Suva products, re-creating an entire business for refrigeration, cleaning agents, propellants, and fire-extinguishing agents. We built seven new manufacturing facilities, gained more than two hundred new patents, and—for good measure—earned an EPA Leadership Award.

We realized extraordinary cost savings by using outside experts instead of developing the expertise in-house. But the most important benefits were our savings in time, energy, and manpower.

Most recently, we have formed a partnership with the chemistry department at the University of North Carolina. With them we have developed brand new catalysts that can create polyolefins. The discovery has led to the largest patent application in the company's history: five hundred claims. If all goes well, we will have the technology commercialized in five years.

Such associations have multiplied our R&D dollars, and the relationships we have formed with people and companies will continue to yield dividends long into the future.

HOLDING THE REINS ON DEVELOPMENT

As we have seen, discovery research flourishes when the structure and control are informal—not bureaucratic—and technical people enjoy a large measure of independence. Once a potential product emerges from the myriad of ideas generated by discovery research, however, we systematically plot its advance to the marketplace, guiding its progress every step of the way.

That approach is relatively new among DuPont's managers, and it owes its popularity to the results of a system we put into effect several years ago. Since then, we have cut average development times in half. At any time, we tackle only 40 percent of the projects we would have taken on in the past, but we support them fully and complete them in about half the time. In one of our businesses, revenue from new products has soared from 5 percent to more than 75 percent of the total, and the dollar amount has grown from $75 million to $450 million.

Our new system, PACE (Product and Cycle Time Excellence), was developed by the Massachusetts firm of Pitiglio, Rabin, Todd, and McGrath. The system relies on multidisciplinary teams to expedite the development of a product or chemical process. The business team acts as a product approval committee that makes sure product development meets scheduled milestones. A PACE engineer oversees the entire process.

By setting forth clear performance criteria, PACE forces fast decisions while compelling managers to assign the right people and fund the project's needs. And because we involve our customers as partners in setting the markers that guide the process, the system helps maintain and strengthen our customer networks. PACE has redefined—as a business process—the development end of the research and development process. Research now plays an integral business role.

INNOVATION OUTSIDE THE LAB

Our commitment to and support for innovation and innovators are by no means limited to what happens in the research laboratory. A variety of awards, rewards, and recognition encourages counterintuitive thinking throughout the corporation. Consider these examples:

• *Legal Department.* Since 1990, the number of lawsuits on file for DuPont has increased from twelve hundred to forty-five hundred. To control our escalating litigation costs, the department managers introduced new, more efficient case-management systems, groupware, and extensive databases that tie DuPont and its outside law firms together in a working network. We have redefined our relationships with those firms, and they now act more like partners than arm's-length vendors. Our counselors from three hundred law firms used to start from scratch each time they took a case to a new state. Now, we have a network of thirty-four primary law firms and four litigation service partners, and we give their cases a running start: material already gathered in the course of trials in other states. We pay each firm on the basis of the value it adds to the presentation of the case.

In its very first year, that approach realized savings of more than $15 million, and we expect to save $20 million more over the next two years. In addition, the average time it takes to bring a case to conclusion is down from thiry-nine to twenty-two months.

• *Human Resources.* Over the years, our human resources people have developed a number of precedent-breaking services to help our employees balance the demands of family and work. In January 1995, we launched Just-In-Time Care. This program helps our employees find care for children, parents, or other dependents whenever unexpected circumstances—illness or bad weather, for example—upset their normal arrangements. It is the first program of its kind in this country.

Last year, a comprehensive survey of eighteen thousand employees showed that people who had considerable family-related responsibilities and made use of our family-resources programs also demonstrated significant increases in their level of commitment to the company. In light of the so-called conventional wisdom that holds that people with major concerns at home are unable or unwilling to put themselves out for the company, these are remarkable findings.

• *Finance Department.* In 1995, we redeemed 156 million shares of common stock worth $8.8 billion from Seagram's. It was the largest stock redemption in history. Our treasury division implemented a financing plan for the redemption that was both fast and innovative.

In contrast to the ten weeks others had needed for an earlier similar effort, our finance people completed the initial financing of the repurchase in only six days. They were able to do that because the company gave our experienced negotiating team special decision-making authority. The team was positioned to tailor options that included allowing investors to select desired maturity dates within a six-month range.

As part of the financing plan, we also sold common stock. A cross-functional team from our accounting, legal, tax, and treasury departments worked with outside accountants and underwriters to obtain approvals from the Securities and Exchange Commission. The team registered the offering in only three days and sold stock both on the open market and to DuPont's pension fund. With 24 million shares the team created a Flexitrust program to fund existing stock-based compensation and benefit plans.

None of this would have been possible without the extensive delegation of authority, the willingness of the team to assume responsibility, and the realization that the team on its own was expected to come up with creative solutions.

BIG THOUGHTS AND IMPOSSIBLE DREAMS

Often innovation takes the form of a succession of small, incremental changes in a product or process. Bright people often focus their intelligence on a discrete stage of a single project and imagine a new way to achieve a small goal.

We all know, however, that there are other sources of innovation. Rare and wonderful, those are the moments of inspiration that redefine a chemical process or give birth to a product with properties no one has ever before imagined. At

DuPont, we seek to nurture innovation of every variety, but like everyone else, I get especially excited when the unexpected occurs.

To spur imaginations and ignite discovery research, we as a company have defined a set of large, "unreachable" goals. Some of those goals do indeed seem unreachable: immortal polymers, zero-waste processes, elastic coatings as hard as diamonds, elastomers as strong as steel, materials that repair themselves, chemical plants that are run by a single chip, and coatings that change color on command.

Nevertheless, we are entirely serious about our support for these "stretch" programs. We publicize them widely throughout the company, expressing our enthusiasm and emphasizing on every possible occasion the critical need for their solutions. The specifics are not as important as the expression of such goals. Goals like these convey an attitude. They encourage all of us to continue our search for Holy Grails as our businesses have defined them over the years. But most important, to my mind, is that these goals tell our people that DuPont is a company that believes in innovation and the future, a company that believes its researchers are extraordinary achievers whose achievements know no limits.

COMPANY PROFILE

E. I. DU PONT DE NEMOURS AND COMPANY, INC.

Business description	Research- and technology-based global chemical and energy company
Founded	1802

Annual sales	$42.2 billion
Annual R&D expenditure	$1.1 billion
R&D as a percent of sales	3%
Net income before taxes	$5.4 billion
Net income after taxes	$3.3 billion
Number of employees worldwide	105,000
Number of employees in R&D	3,600

TOP DUPONT PRODUCTS

Apparel

Coolmax

Dacron polyester

Lycra brand spandex

MicroMattique microdenier polyester

Nylon

Thermax

Construction

Butacite window interlayer

Corian solid surface material for countertops, shower stalls, etc.

Hypalon synthetic rubber for roofing

Mylar polyester solar films

Suva refrigerants

Tedlar PVF film

Teflon fluoropolymer resin for wire insulation

Tefzel fluoropolymer resin film

Ti-Pure titanium dioxide

Tyvek spunbonded olefin housewrap

Electronics

Birox resistors for hybrid microcircuits

Crastin PBT thermoplastic polyester

Fodel photoprintable thick films

Kapton polyimide film

Mylar polyester film

Pyralux flexible laminates

Riston dry film photo resists

Rynite PET thermoplastic polyester

Teflon fluoropolymer film

Zenite liquid crystal polymers

Zytel HTN (high-temperature nylon)

Agriculture and Food-Related Products

Herbicides

Ally—wheat

Basis—corn

Harmony Extra—wheat, barley, and oats

Londax—rice

Matrix—potatoes

Staple—cotton

Synchrony STS or Reliance STS—soybeans

Upbeet—sugar beets

Optimum Quality Grains for high-oil corn and soybeans

Packaging materials for liquids, meats, cheeses, and snacks

Crystar PET resin

Riboprinter Microbial Characterization system

Selar PT barrier resins

Surlyn ionomer resin

Home Products

Antron nylon for carpets

Corian solid surface material

Dacron polyester fiberfill products for pillows and comforters

Comforel

Thermalite

Thermaloft

Quallofil

Silverstone and Silverstone Extra

Stainmaster certified stain-resistant carpeting

Stainmaster Grand Luxura

Stainmaster Xtra Life

Suva refrigerants

Tynex nylon filaments for toothbrushes and paintbrushes

Leisure

Cordura nylon for backpacks, luggage, hiking boots, and activewear

Delrin acetal resin

Kevlar aramid fiber for sails, boats

Zytel ST (super-tough) nylon

Printing and Publishing

Crosfield Celiz platesetter

Crosfield electronic imaging products

Cyrel photopolyester plates

Digital WaterProof PreView system

Safety

Kevlar aramid fiber for bullet-resistant vests, cut-resistant gloves and
clothing

Nomex aramid fiber for firefighter turnout coats, protective garments

Sontara spunlaced fabric for hospital operating room gowns and drapes

Transportation

Antron nylon for automotive upholstery

Bexloy automotive engineering resins

Butacite polyvinyl butyral window interlayer

Hytrel polyester elastomer

Kapton film for satellites

Kevlar aramid fiber pulp as asbestos replacement in brake linings

Krytox specialty lubricants

Nomex aramid fiber for flame- and smoke-resistant aircraft upholstery

Nomex honeycomb for aircraft floors

Suva refrigerants

Teflon fluoropolymer for aerospace wire and cable

Vespel polyimide parts for aerospace engines

Viton fluoroelastomer

In the next few years, the global economy will provide new opportunities but also a much more competitive business environment. Our response will be continuing change at DuPont. We intend to be the leading company in our major businesses in all our global markets.

What strategies will guide the changes that take place? Our basic strategy to grow shareholder value is straightforward: profitable growth by focusing on what we do best. We intend to grow our strongest businesses globally. Research and new technology will continue to be the major source of competitive advantage providing improved processes and new products. . . . We will drive year-to-year improvements in the productivity of all resources employed. And we will differentiate ourselves by executing faster and more effectively than our competitors.

We intend to create our own future.

**Edgar S. Woolard, Jr., Chairman of the Board and
John A. Krol, President and Chief Executive Officer
1995 Annual Report**

Fact: DuPont's first exports went to Spain in 1805.

Fact: As early as 1909, DuPont was investigating synthetic fibers, and in 1927 it launched its fundamental research program, starting the 20th century's materials revolution.

Fact: Since 1987, DuPont chemicals and specialties businesses have reduced airborne carcinogens and toxins by more than two-thirds in the United States and about one-half globally.

Fact: DuPont has developed a technique for recycling used carpeting into nylon resin, from which automotive components may be manufactured.

General Electric Company

"Set goals for succeeding generations."

DR. LEWIS S. EDELHEIT
SENIOR VICE PRESIDENT

In 1969, a graduate of the University of Illinois, I went to work on X-ray systems at the General Electric Research and Development Center in Schenectady, New York. It was America's first industrial research lab, the legacy of Thomas A. Edison, the father of innovation.

I had been at GE for only a few years when a British company, EMI, developed the CAT scanner, a device that would revolutionize medical diagnosis. As a leading manufacturer of X-ray equipment, GE was worried. Nevertheless, we didn't get too excited until hospitals around the country started spending their X-ray budgets on CAT scanners. Even then, I remember, we moved slowly.

In those days, GE's corporate Research and Development Center acted as if it had all the time in the world. And cost was the least of our concerns. We were a stand-alone organization, and we were confident that our researchers would eventually create something wonderful in the ivory tower of our laboratories. In the past, GE labs had always come up with the technology that was needed to, say, make jet engines quieter, or plastics more heat-resistant. The guys in research would hand the technology over to an advanced engineering group of the appropriate business. The engineers there would build a test prototype and pass that along to design and production.

In those days, people on the business side worried about manufacturability and price. We in the labs shared more common ground with our competitors' researchers than with people in our own businesses. And though the whole process was slow and often expensive, we were confident. Our unique capabilities often enabled us to achieve performance the competition could not match.

The change in attitude since then has been monumental. Recognizing that today's business environment is no longer conducive to that old model, we have transformed virtually every facet of our research operation: how we define our goals, structure our management, relate with suppliers—we've even changed the way we finance our work.

Today's researchers function in a world of exploding technology and imploding organizations, and the widespread proliferation of technology around the world has transformed technology into what sometimes appears to be nearly a commodity. The proprietary edge performance breakthroughs provide is short-lived indeed.

GE's ability to attract world-class researchers and fund technology developments is no longer sufficient to sustain its unique position as an industry leader. We realize that more and more companies are able to match our skills. So first we learned to be faster than the competition, but it didn't take long to discover that speed alone wouldn't be enough to save us, because when we went for speed, everybody else did, too. When everyone else mastered speed, we emphasized reducing costs. That's when price became everything, and we stood by and watched as others who failed to reduce their costs struggled.

FORGING A CULTURE OF BOUNDARYLESS COOPERATION

How does a corporate research lab achieve simultaneous and continuous improvements in performance, speed, cost, and quality? At GE, we do that by emphasizing what our chairman and CEO, Jack Welch, calls "the soft stuff." We work hard to eliminate the artificial boundaries that separate the various aspects of the larger enterprise.

In the old days, when engineers handed drawings to the manufacturing people, the manufacturing people would ask, "How do we know it works?" The engineers, should they deign to answer, would say, "Because we say so." Of course, the manufacturing people had to counter, and would reply, "We don't believe you. Don't bother us until you can give us a completely finished drawing with every possible annotation. It's not clear to us that you have any idea what you're doing."

Horizontal turf boundaries like those impede communication and slow response time. And vertical boundaries—rigid layer upon layer of bureaucracy—also inhibit productivity. Back in the old days, we snaked through endless reviews of engineering designs. People checked their projects with their bosses, who would then turn around to check them with their bosses, all the way up and down the line. As long as people continued to make their numbers and achieved some level of success, nobody prevented them from ignoring or snubbing the expertise or authority of other groups of people.

Today, such behavior is just plain impossible. GE aims to be a company without boundaries. In practice, that means we are continually organizing cross-functional innovation teams that include representatives from research, marketing, manufacturing, engineering, and service, as well as vendors and customers.

Two years ago, we introduced an electrodeless screw-in fluorescent lamp that matches the volume and lighting quality of its competitors but uses only a third as much electric power and lasts significantly longer. The innovation team responsible for that product came up with remarkable results, and they achieved success against daunting odds.

Under usual circumstances, members of such teams work in a single location. We are most effective if we have our team members sitting—as we say—around one coffee pot, even if that requires spending a few months in a Wisconsin motel in the dead of winter.

In this case, however, the requisite groups were scattered around the globe: the people responsible for overall design were in Great Britain; manufacturing was scheduled in Hungary; and the group that would develop the electronic ballast was in Ohio. The team members worked together, bridging the physical distances with regular phone calls, e-mail, video conferences, and extended visits in one or another of the project locations.

The research lab was the glue that held the operation together. It developed and distributed the data, and the data enabled the team to select the materials and determine the lamp's design and dimensions. In addition, the lab provided the scientific understanding that helped iron out differences among team members.

Work-Out is another GE innovation. From time to time, members of the lamp team met at locations remote from the factory and the laboratory. Such meetings have a stated specific purpose. People attend, knowing that they will have opportunities to express their ideas freely and the rest of the team will give them a fair hearing. Experience has taught us that once people realize the Work-Outs are for real, they gain self-confidence, and the sessions become extremely productive.

The goal of such a session is to create a small-company mentality in an organization that is clearly anything but small. GE employs about 220,000 people. That total includes about 8,500 scientists and engineers, 12 percent of whom work at our Research and Development Center. About 500 of the R&D Center's technologists have doctorates.

Bigness does, of course, have its benefits, and synergy is

one of them. When researchers shop their ideas around the company, strange and unexpected marriages of convenience occur. Technology from lighting and lasers became the basis of a new X-ray detector. Coating and machining techniques created for the aircraft-engine business were applied to power generators.

Bigness has its advantages, all right, but too often size proves a hindrance. It's difficult for us to match the speed and vitality of small entrepreneurial companies. Bigness breeds bureaucracy, and emphasis shifts from speed to control, leading to managing, and from serving the customer to serving the bureaucracy. Over the last few years, GE has engaged in an ongoing struggle to clear away bureaucracy and keep new barriers from forming.

In the process of clearing away the bureaucratic structure, we confirmed that those people who are close to a particular job invariably know it better than those who are one or two layers removed from the action. We developed Work-Out to make sure that we heard from the people who have crucial experience and knowledge. We took those people from all parts of the company and assigned them to our cross-functional innovation teams. And they really produced.

A few years ago, for example, our Power Systems business was preparing to bid on some big orders in China and India. We assembled a team of engineers, marketers, and financial people to redesign our 660-megawatt steam turbine-generator. Over the course of several decades, we had been improving it incrementally. But the work of that team was anything but incremental. In record time, that team managed to trim the machine's weight by a million pounds, cut its length by 20 percent, and reduce its cost considerably.

Because our research center is home to all kinds of scientists—chemists, computer scientists, systems engineers, metallurgists, and so forth—we have no problem assembling highly capable multidisciplinary teams to tackle our complex projects, and our determination to reinvent GE as a hungry, market-driven entrepreneurial company has altered the way we underwrite this research center. We used to draw two-thirds of our funding from an assessment on the company as a whole, and the remainder was from contracts with individual GE businesses or outside customers. Today, 75 percent of the funding is from contracts, and company-wide assessments account for only a quarter of the total.

We are no longer isolated in the ivory tower of research. Contract funding keeps us much closer to the realities of the market. When our clients—both internal and external—feel market pressures, so do we. Because our efforts are financially integrated at the business level, we are now in touch with GE's customers and their needs. If our GE customers don't think we can produce results in a cost-effective way, they don't have to fund us. That is the best measure of our value to GE.

Another more traditional way to measure the success of a company's research operations is the number of inventions it claims. In 1995, the U.S. Patent and Trademark Office issued GE 962 U.S. patents, ranking it seventh among all companies worldwide. The R&D Center got about a third of the GE patents.

A change in the marketplace has necessitated a redefinition of the roles of research and researchers here at GE. In addition to the businesses bringing us their ideas, our researchers often come up with their own new product notions, which they shop around the company. In effect, our researchers need to be entrepreneurs as well as innovators. They play a direct role in bringing technology from the lab to the marketplace.

In today's fiercely competitive environment, where speed-to-market is the chief measure of success, it helps to have a head start. That's what GE is trying to accomplish by planning two or three product generations ahead. We organize our projects to yield a successful product and—generation by generation—provide for its improvement.

When we first assembled innovation teams, we told them, "You used to have three years to build a new washing machine or new CAT scanner. Today's world is moving much too fast for that. You've got eighteen months." Given such tight deadlines, the teams naturally shied away from radically new approaches: They played it safe with technically risk-free solutions. After a while we couldn't even be sure the teams would tell us about any startling new ideas for really improving performance. I guess the most egregious result of this cautious approach was that by the end of that eighteen months, our so-called solution would already be out of date. We'd scramble to assemble yet another innovation team, assign it the same down-and-dirty project, and again require results within eighteen months. I don't need to tell you how ineffective that was.

Now we take a multigeneration approach to product development. That approach helps us keep the technology risk low for the first generation while preparing us for the changing future. Right from the beginning, we set goals for succeeding generations. Because the research lab has a window on technological change around the world, and because the lab is now a full partner on the business team, we are beautifully positioned to take a leading role from one generation of a product to the next.

Here's how the multigenerational approach works. The team determines for generation two, twenty-four months out, and generation three, thirty-six months out, how we need to proceed. We specify the necessary advances in technology, product, performance, funding, and quality. Often we try to forecast ideas about a new platform four years out. Our critical responsibility—even while full-scale development of the first generation is under way—is to fund research and development that reduces risk for those subsequent product generations.

It's only when we clearly and thoroughly understand our customers' needs that we can develop successful multiyear plans. In the case of the long-range plan that evolved for GE Transportation Systems' locomotives, we had to recognize the limits of power. We could never have produced satisfactory products if we had simply cranked out progressively more powerful engines. At some point the engines would be too powerful, and the wheels of the locomotives would spin on the tracks. Our researchers are currently developing the know-how to solve that problem. Because we had developed control software that alerted us to the conditions under which the locomotive wheels would slip, we were able to prepare for corrective action.

Control technology comprises many elements. Some we already know how to employ. Others are both more sophisticated and riskier. The key to multigenerational planning is to incorporate elements gradually, so that by the time such elements are introduced we will have reduced the risks to acceptable levels.

Our proficiency in control technology didn't come about by chance. We have contributed to the multigenerational plans of many different businesses, and the cumulative experience has built a critical mass of expertise. We have applied that expertise to GE's business in aircraft engines, motors, and appliances, to name only a few.

We design every multigenerational plan with low cost and high quality at its core. Our market-back approach calls for us to define, up front, a package of performance specifications, and we set costs in accordance with what our surveys and focus groups tell us customers will pay.

In a cost-based development project, our technology-plus-business perspective is a noteworthy asset. Recently we assembled a team to develop an industrial product. The project manager was from a GE business, and our researchers worked directly with manufacturing people and vendors. Our lab contributed not only to the product's design and manufacturing but also to the Underwriters Laboratories' certification process, training the sales force, and preparing manuals. When I reflect upon the role a researcher used to assume in this process, it's hard to understand how or why we used to ignore such critical aspects of the product development process.

I have also learned that when we involve suppliers in the process, we're able to get a much better handle on the actual risks and costs of a particular project. I advocate giving suppliers both product specifications and cost targets. They know that it's in their best interest—as well as ours—to find the best low-cost approach. At GE we give our suppliers an ever-broadening role in our technological life.

Not that long ago, none of us doubted that vertical integration would provide the solution to any problem. If we needed new technology, we would create it ourselves. But in today's high-speed business environment, we know better. Today we develop technology for the sake of competitive advantage, but we no longer believe we need to be omnipotent. If we know that suppliers already own the technology we need, we don't bother wasting time and resources to duplicate their capabilities.

One challenge in relying on suppliers for certain technology is maintaining our touch with up-to-date technology. If we don't remain sophisticated enough to understand their technologies completely, we won't get the most out of our partnerships, and we can't be sure that the final product will meet the established specifications. Furthermore, by being on top of the latest technologies, we can contribute enormously to our suppliers' efforts. My staff and I work hard to make sure we take full advantage of the collective knowledge of our people.

GRASSROOTS QUALITY CONTROL

The research lab plays a huge role in keeping product development costs down and quality high. Our responsibility extends all the way to the factory floor, where our goal is to create the best match between part tolerance and process variability.

For example, in our plant that manufactures moving parts for aircraft engines, specially trained workers use lasers to drill one hundred minute holes in a metal airfoil only a few centimeters long. There is no margin for error.

We could have hired hundreds of quality control inspectors, but we realized that we would get better results if we trained the workers on the floor to monitor their own work. We designed a systematic process that alerts the operators to any aberration. When the laser machine starts to drift, workers know soon enough to act quickly and keep the lasers from straying beyond the tight tolerance specifications.

How did we do that? We kept our eyes open, saw a need, and filled it. Our management science researchers have developed expert methods for catching timely data on the fly, analyzing the information instantaneously, and displaying understandable results for quick-response adjustments. Since we developed the systems that keep the laser drilling and other aircraft-engine manufacturing processes on track, we have cut manufacturing losses by 20 to 70 percent.

Does it seem peculiar that our top-rated scientists and engineers immerse themselves in cost accounting, manufacturing, and marketing? It shouldn't. They do and they must.

Our technical work is useful and effective only to the extent that it keeps our customers' businesses alive and vibrant in the marketplace. Of course, our work must be of the highest quality. Our researchers deliver on time and on budget. Few other laboratories can match that performance. Because innovation research is, almost by definition, expensive, many corporations—particularly those that failed to embrace cost and time imperatives—can no longer support their own research facilities. Many labs around the world have either shrunk or disappeared in recent years because they failed to stay current.

Every innovative enterprise faces an unending succession of choices. Which projects should we undertake? How can we measure one project against another? Do we know enough to determine which projects are vital and which will lead us to a dead end?

First, let me say that my job is *not* to be the person who makes *every* one of those decisions. I don't sit at my desk processing proposals from the lab, awarding some a go-ahead and sentencing others to the dustbin. No single person can always be right. And GE is huge. That's why we have three or four simultaneous selection processes, each with its own philosophy and staff. Each staff assesses the proposed and ongoing projects, and we compare their various judgments to find the best answer.

There are a number of criteria at work in each of these processes. Determining the right mix of projects is akin to managing a personal investment portfolio. Prudent investors keep a certain portion of their assets safe in cash or, perhaps, government bonds. By that same token, many of our projects are short-term, low-risk, and aim to satisfy a clearly identified need: for example, improvements to already successful products. And just as investors might put most of the balance of their money in blue chips, we devote a good portion of our resources to creating new products that complement and supplement existing product lines. The risk is substantial, but multigenerational planning controls that risk.

Investors who are looking for a possible home run also assign a portion of their assets to risky, high-odds bets. Our long-term, open-ended projects have the highest possible risk with the potential for extremely rewarding payoff. Those projects are the game-changers, such as GE's Lexan polycarbonate resin, DuPont's nylon, and Bell's transistor.

Management would be apt to lose patience if research were to undertake too many ultra-high-risk projects. Because in every research situation, whether the goal is a game-changer or a modified gadget, the greatest danger is not that we might fail, but that we might waste time and resources on inconsequential projects.

You should know that my emphasis on vitalness (i.e., not wasting time on nonvital work) is neither easy to maintain nor popular. Imagine, if you can, scientists who, after several months of first-rate research, learn that we have to cancel their projects due to considerations beyond their control: Perhaps the company wants to embark upon a joint venture in the same field; maybe we need to cut costs, or the market has changed, or by chance one of our suppliers has suddenly come up with a better solution. Our scientists can't complete their work, publish it, or see it to production. That's no fun for anyone, most especially the scientists. I have to admit that I myself get pretty upset when one of my projects suddenly gets canceled because our customer has changed strategy. But if we don't react appropriately and quickly to the rapidly changing technical and business environment, we condemn ourselves to seeming irrelevant at best and, at worst, unresponsive to our customers' needs.

GE challenges its researchers to perform effectively in a boundaryless environment. We are all reminded, nearly every day, just how difficult that is. We reward those who show boundaryless leadership. They merit increases in salary and incentive compensation. At a memorable quarterly meeting of our Corporate Executive Council—the heads of the businesses and the senior corporate management—Jack Welch commended a couple of staff members for their exemplary boundaryless behavior. He handed each of them a big check right on the spot. By contrast, on several rather public occasions, Welch also emphasized that certain fairly high-level people had lost their jobs because they lacked the skills to lead in a boundaryless environment.

That failure loomed large before Welch's eyes. Those people had been making their numbers, but he considered their leadership ineffective. They had built walls between organizations; they didn't heed other people's best practices; and they failed to adopt new ideas. In short, the word *innovation* was not in their vocabulary.

BOUNDARY BREAKER

I spend a great deal of my time out in the businesses. I participate in loads of meetings with representatives from manufacturing, engineering, and marketing, and I bring along people from our labs.

At such meetings or wherever I am, if I happen to overhear somebody say, "Manufacturing won't put enough people on this program," or "Engineering still hasn't firmed up its design. We can't possibly go into manufacturing," it is part of my job to help to force those issues to resolution.

As a result, I occasionally upset my people. As R&D chief, it is my job to go beyond representing the lab. I represent the General Electric Company, and it's everybody's job to break down boundaries. Boundary-busting is how I spend the bulk of my time and energy.

I have organized our labs with a commitment to blurring traditional boundaries and ensuring that the work we do is vital. Each of our thirteen labs has a different technical focus—mechanical engineering or chemistry, for example—and our ten business interface managers are responsible for making sure that the labs are doing work that is vital to our company.

The business interface managers work with one or two of the company's businesses and try to make sure that the work in the labs matches business needs. Their goal is to expedite commercialization of our laboratory results.

In such a large organization, it's not easy to keep track of what everyone is doing. That's why I have insisted on meetings and forums so that laboratory managers can share their best practices and better learn the lessons of boundaryless cooperation. Because if we don't learn our lessons, it's the customer who ends up paying the price.

Consider the following scenario: An internal customer in our aircraft-engine business tells one of our mechanical engineers, "We can't seem to find an effective glue that holds under all circumstances. I don't know what we'll do." The mechanical engineer tries to help but is unsuccessful.

A few months later, I find myself in conversation with the aircraft-engine customer and first learn of the problem.

"Who were you talking to?" I ask.

"Mechanical engineering."

"Why weren't you talking to our chemists if you needed an adhesive?"

"How should I know about your chemists? Nobody ever suggested another resource."

Such are the conversations that try my soul. I'm confident that our people now understand that we must not construct boundaries within our company. I've beaten them over the head with this message, repeating it at regular meetings, special meetings, encounters with supervisors, and at the

Corporate Leadership Institute where people from different levels and businesses convene. They now know that the person who fails to think in terms of the best solution for the company as a whole will be penalized.

Now that you're familiar with the elements of GE's research operation—encouraging boundaryless teamwork, planning multigenerationally, and meeting the simultaneous demands of speed, quality, and low cost—you may be wondering how all these pieces work together.

Consider our new line of Profile clothes washers. GE Appliances led the Profile development program, but the team included researchers and suppliers as well as design, engineering, manufacturing, marketing, and service people from our business operation. At the research lab, our role was to apply science and mathematical modeling to reduce costs, enhance quality, and promote performance improvements.

A perennial problem with washing machines is noisy shaking on owners' floors. Our mathematical models helped us design a suspension that keeps shaking to a minimum, and our physics-based models dictated design considerations for significant improvements to the agitator's transmission. State-of-the-art fluid mechanics modeling methods—similar to those used in designing jet engines—defined a new design for the agitator's vane. Based on mathematical considerations, our researchers were even able to improve the shape of the fabric-softener dispenser. The new dispenser empties its contents during the spin cycle, and no residue remains.

That's a clean example of how we do business in our lab

these days. And that's how we manage innovation today. As innovators, we continually subject what we do to review, modification, or even cancellation, depending on marketplace activity. In today's competitive climate, nobody can afford to relax.

Not long ago, one of our internal customers called me to complain about something. I have to confess, the complaint seemed fairly insignificant to me, but I assured the customer I would take care of it. Over the next few weeks, the same customer called with similar no-problem complaints. Each time I investigated, I found the claim to be unfounded. Still, the customer called. I couldn't figure out why this customer was harassing me!

Finally, the light dawned. Behind all the noise, the customer was delivering a simple message: Pay attention to me. Let me know you'll listen to me. Today, if we at GE are to remain in the vanguard of innovation—in the laboratories and everywhere else—we always need to keep our customers' needs our number-one priority.

COMPANY PROFILE

GENERAL ELECTRIC COMPANY

Business description	Diversified technology, manufacturing, and services company
Founded	1878
Annual sales	$70,028 billion
Annual R&D expenditure	$1.9 billion
R&D as a percent of sales	2.7%

Net income before taxes	$9,737 billion
Net income after taxes	$6,573 billion
Number of employees worldwide	222,000
Number of employees in R&D	8,000 (includes engineers)

GENERAL ELECTRIC'S HISTORY OF INNOVATION

1900 to 1910

Process for making the ductile tungsten filament: Filling a lamp bulb with an jnert gas at atmospheric pressure, rather than operating the filament in a vacuum, resulted in a 20 percent improvement.

1910 to 1920

Irving Langmuir's studies of the chemistry of surfaces led to his winning a Nobel Prize for chemistry; invention of the modern medical X-ray tube.

1920 to 1930

First U.S. television broadcasts; improved processes for making cemented tungsten carbide.

1930 to 1940

Process for making the key building blocks of silicones; first million-volt X-ray tube for commercial applications.

1940 to 1950

Electronic countermeasures to enemy radar systems; invention of modern combustor for turbojet planes.

1950 to 1960

Process for synthetic industrial diamonds; LEXAN resin; new methods for making plastics.

1960 to 1970

Ivar Giaever's discovery of superconductive tunneling led to his share of the 1973 Nobel Prize for physics; MultiVapor lamp for outdoor and stadium lighting.

1970 to 1980

Fan-beam computed tomography medical X-ray scanner; ULTEM high-performance plastics.

1980 to 1990

Gem quality diamonds, which are the world's best conductors of heat; magnetic resonance imager for medical diagnostics; industrial automation technologies including computed tomography X-ray inspection system for manufactured parts and high-power lasers for drilling holes in superalloys.

1990 to present

Genura compact fluorescent bulb with light quality of an incandescent; fully digital LOGIQ 700 ultrasound system; management-science and artificial intelligence applications for GE Capital Services; first magnetic resonance scanner that allows physicians to stand and work with patients during scanning.

We describe our emerging culture by an awkward but descriptive term: "boundaryless.". . .

The sweetest fruit of boundaryless behavior has been the demise of "Not-Invested-Here" and its utter disappearance from our company. We quickly began to learn from each other: productivity from Lighting; "quick response" asset management from Appliances; transaction effectiveness from GE Capital; the application of "bullet-train" cost-reduction techniques from Aircraft Engines; and global account management from Plastics—just to name a few. At the same time, we embarked on an endless search for ideas from the great companies of the world. Wal-Mart taught us the direct customer feedback technique we call Quick Market Intelligence. We learned New Product Introduction methods from Toshiba, Chrysler, and Hewlett-Packard, and advanced manufacturing techniques from American Standard, Toyota, and Yokogawa. AlliedSignal, Ford, and Xerox shared their insights into launching a quality initiative. Motorola, which created a dramatically successful, quality-focused culture over a period of a decade, has been more than generous in sharing its experiences with us.

John F. Welch, Jr., Chairman of the Board and Chief Executive Officer
Paolo Fresco, Vice Chairman of the Board and Executive Officer
John D. Opie, Vice Chairman of the Board and Executive Officer
1995 Annual Report

Fact: On the 100th anniversary of the Dow Jones Industrial Average, GE was the only company to have been on the list since its origin.

Fact: GE is the world's largest producer of large and small jet engines for commercial and military aircraft.

Fact: GE manufactures more than half of the diesel freight locomotives purchased in North America, and its locomotives run in seventy-five countries worldwide.

Pfizer Inc.

"The long-term winners are those that provide quality *and* value."

WILLIAM C. STEERE, JR.
CHAIRMAN AND CHIEF EXECUTIVE OFFICER

WITH
DR. JOHN NIBLACK
SENIOR VICE PRESIDENT, RESEARCH AND DEVELOPMENT

To most outsiders, our company may seem strange and confusing. Pfizer is, after all, extraordinary. In fiscal 1996, our investment in research and development totaled $1.7 billion. That's 14 percent of sales. Hoping—yes, *hoping*—that our R&D will yield at least a few new marketable products, we make a comparable investment every year. And we do not follow the growth-by-acquisition path most other companies in our industry have taken. Even though most of the pharmaceutical industry is undergoing intense consolidation, Pfizer remains steadfastly independent.

Our industry, like so many others these days, is struggling through a period of unprecedented turmoil. People from every part of the world, from every level of society, and from all cultures are questioning whether the old ways of delivering health-care services are still valid.

In certain countries, generic medications are proliferating, and impudent patent pirates continue to prosper, unpunished. Nobody doubts that competition within the pharmaceutical industry will continue to intensify, particularly here in the United States. With increasing numbers of private physicians—traditionally the gatekeepers of the marketplace—joining managed care organizations, passive players in the pharmaceutical industry are learning that only the aggressive actors will survive.

To compound the severity of our industry's predicament, the cost of doing business has skyrocketed. To gain Food and Drug Administration (FDA) approval for even one new medication, we can easily spend more than $500 million. That's ten times what it cost only two decades ago. And these days, we're tackling diseases like Alzheimer's and AIDS-related infections, which are considerably more complex than those we've taken on in the past. Therefore, the tools of our trade are comparably more elaborate and, by extension, expensive. For example, at least a third of today's research and development projects involve recombinant DNA technology and molecular genetics.

In theory, I suppose, we at Pfizer could decide to take a breather, cut back our research costs, and pray that the products we already have in the pipeline will sustain the company for awhile. Would it be so bad if we concentrated simply on enhancing the drugs we have in our product line? Wouldn't that be a way to minimize risk? More than a few of our competitors are doing that. To my mind, neither approach is viable.

Pfizer's market—global health care—is far too demanding

to take either of those approaches. We have intensified our push to discover and develop clinically unprecedented therapies. I am proud to report that our research expenses are rising at a substantially higher rate than sales.

I am convinced, and the record to date supports me, that the only way to survive and prosper in this business is to give our researchers the resources they need to produce a steady flow of new medicines. But let me assure you that we don't simply throw money at our chemists and hope for the best.

MANAGING INNOVATION

I know for a fact that there are companies in our industry that take a different approach from ours. They hire talented young scientists, give them the equipment they say they need, offer a bit of direction—"We'd like you to focus on antibiotics research"—and wait to see what happens. Pfizer does not work that way. At Pfizer, we *manage* innovation.

Most colleges don't teach their students how to function in an applied-research environment. While it's true that college students might take great courses in organic chemistry, course work can give students only the theoretical background for undertaking drug-discovery research. College courses don't prepare students to cope with the frustrations of spending a whole career focused on a task that never yields a new medicine. Nor do they equip people to work as members of a multidisciplinary team like those Pfizer assembles to achieve its ambitious goals.

Because of our world renown, Pfizer is able to select its

researchers from among the top young PhDs. We assign each recruit to one of our drug project teams. The managers of our teams are themselves veterans of successful team efforts. We have found that for the most part they are extremely effective communicators, passing management's best practices from one generation of scientists to the next.

Of course, Pfizer's best practices have evolved over many years, but nobody considers them inviolable or unimprovable. We want all our people to develop and implement new and better ways of managing. At the same time, we have not been subject to frequent turnover in our management ranks, and we do not import outside managers. Over the last thirty years, every one of our research directors has risen through company ranks, giving our research efforts a valuable sense of continuity. At Pfizer, there is an institutional memory that supports the way we solve problems and organize our work.

In some ways, managing innovation is analogous to breaking in a spirited horse. You are never sure of success until you achieve your goal. In the meantime, everyone takes a few lumps.

THE UNCERTAIN PATH TOWARD INVENTION

At Pfizer, the process of invention follows a well-worn path. It begins when a company scientist, typically a chemist or pharmacologist, introduces an idea for a new drug. We classify such ideas as approaches. The science of a particular approach, its staffing, and its financial requirements are set forth in a project operating plan, which senior scientists and research managers examine and critique. If they approve the plan, we assemble multidisciplinary teams to plan and manage the next research stage, which includes the development of biological screens and animal models. Those teams stay with the project, continually asking the penultimate question: Based on progress to date and our knowledge of our competition, should we continue to underwrite this idea?

Some projects do lead to the discovery of a compound that demonstrates all the desired characteristics. We consider such a compound a drug candidate, and we submit it to comprehensive animal and limited human testing. The performance data from those tests—effectiveness and side effects—become the focus of a new advanced candidate management team, which first determines whether the candidate will be a marketable product. Of course, that team includes a marketing representative.

The team studies competing products already on the market and asks, "Will our candidate have much of an advantage?" We also consider drugs competing companies are working on and ask, "Are they ahead of us or behind us? How do the side effects of their product compare with our candidate's?" Many of Pfizer's competitors postpone such marketing considerations to a much later stage in their process.

If our candidate continues to show promise, we consider elevating it from the research phase to the development stage. It is during the development stage that each candidate is subjected to years of enormously expensive clinical testing involving ten thousand or more patients. The test stage is grueling, but it is exciting, too. Everyone knows—and hopes—that successful completion of these tests precedes FDA approval.

The central research division's staff of forty-six hundred conducts that complex process. More than half of those people work in the million square feet of laboratories at the division's headquarters in Groton, Connecticut. Most of the others work in laboratories in Sandwich, Great Britain, and Nagoya, Japan. All told, the central research division employs about 10 percent of Pfizer's entire workforce.

They are a painstaking, patient crew, and they have to be. The mathematics of drug research is discouraging: Only half of the approaches to new drugs end up as candidates; only 20 percent of the candidates reach the development process; and only 10 percent of those in development ever reach the marketplace. In other words, just 1 percent of our ideas ever sees the light of day. That's the bottom line of a process that takes from ten to fifteen years.

At Pfizer, we track our progress with a variety of benchmarks. We aim to launch at least one major product annually. So, given the disheartening mathematics, we know that means we need to consider no fewer than one hundred approaches every year; we know also that at least ten candidates must reach the development phase. The measure of our success at that level is the number of products for which we have filed an Investigational New Drug Application with the FDA. Approval of that application is the permit for human experimentation.

Our research and development people have prepared many more promising candidates for release in the late 1990s and beyond than any other company in our industry. That is the true measure of Pfizer's success.

PLACING YOUR BETS

Are you wondering at what point we actually begin to manage the process of innovation? For us, innovation is an integral part of the process that leads to one of the one hundred approaches we work on each year. There are several possible bases for those first-stage choices.

Consider osteoarthritis. The available therapies leave most patients dissatisfied; they simply do not prevent long-term bone and joint degeneration. Just about everybody suffers from the disease during old age, but many people are afflicted much earlier in their lives. Finding a new medication for osteoarthritis seems like a natural. Right?

We don't make our decisions that way. First we might inquire whether there are any new ideas about how and why the disease occurs. Do we have any new knowledge concerning the disease's progress? If the answers to these questions are negative, we discourage our scientists from spending their time and energies on possible new treatments. In the case of osteoarthritis, the answers to these questions continue to discourage us.

By definition, the success of applied research depends on breakthroughs in basic research. We could possibly prime the pump by undertaking basic research ourselves. Many pharmaceutical companies do, even though fundamental research may take five or ten years. Nevertheless, a company that is first to capitalize on a breakthrough can push products to market in a year or two. We at Pfizer choose not to add more years to what is already a brutally long innovation cycle.

Also, basic research by definition must be less focused and less manageable than the kind of applied research we do at Pfizer. Its payoff for us is therefore even more uncertain, and its rewards are too often irrelevant.

Although we don't force the science at Pfizer, we do collaborate with outside research partners who are engaged in cutting-edge investigations. Pharmaceutical research and knowledge are making enormous strides, moving forward at a phenomenal rate. We consider it imperative to stay alert and abreast of the latest developments.

Scientists have successfully isolated individual genes in order to study just how each one operates within the body. Subsequent research describes chemical processes within those individual genes. Say they can detail how a gene associated with breast cancer produces a particular protein. That information sets the stage for our people to design a drug that can block production of that protein. Our researchers regularly refer to the huge computer databases that store the results of basic research on hundreds of genes.

The advent of molecular genetics has given our researchers a wealth of new science to explore, and that, naturally, has had its effects on our decision-making process. Our selection process grows increasingly aggressive, and because there are so many *superior* proposals, those that are only perfectly fine stand no chance.

RESEARCH IS A BUSINESS

Shaping all our decisions is one crucial truth: We are a business. Marketability must always play a critical role in the approval process. Scientific viability is only one of the hurdles that separates an idea from administrative sanction. Is the unmet need for the proposed product substantial? Compared with another approach in a related field, how effectively will the proposed product meet that need? At this stage of the approval process, we might use a matrix model to plot a proposal's odds of making its way through the R&D process against the odds of its being a big-payout product.

We invoke matrix techniques in corporate decision-making throughout Pfizer. Our research division is not an ivory tower; it is considered—because, of course, it is—one of our business divisions. Its annual budget is almost $2 billion a year. Pfizer makes its living *selling* pharmaceuticals. We cannot afford to chase any leads—no matter how intriguing—that are unlikely to pay off. If a project starts to founder, we end it. Fast.

In our research division, just as in the rest of the corporation, we emphasize speed. In order to facilitate our processes, we have reduced the number of management levels that separate the sales force and research chemists from the chairman. As senior management people retire or resign, we no longer replace them. We want to eliminate bureaucratic impediments to fast decision-making and immediate action. We want to move power down through the organization.

We are also extending our reach beyond our corporate walls, to establish relationships with dozens of small organizations on the leading edge of research in such areas as viruses, bacteria, and certain genes. As big and talented as our corporate research team is, today's fast-paced advances are too diverse and dynamic for any one organization to handle alone.

Our scientists manage the collaborative relationships we forge with small companies. Many of our partner companies are run by young, aggressive entrepreneurs who need capital but have no use for a corporate partner that aims to trample them. We at Pfizer have spent plenty of energy learning to work effectively with entrepreneurial companies, and it's already been worth the effort. The best and brightest newcomers come to us with their ideas. Ultimately, of course, each of those partnerships needs to bear fruit. Whenever we determine that the work of one of those companies seems to have no commercial potential, we drop it from our portfolio and replace it with one that looks more promising.

Some of our competitors have addressed the need to be close to basic research by acquiring or merging with companies that have desirable capabilities. I believe that such a strategy causes more problems than it solves. All too often, the top managers and scientists who owned equity in the acquired company take their new wealth and leave. And it's an enormous challenge to happily marry two previously independent organizations. Turf wars and anxiety about the future distract attention and energy from the important research, which, as I mentioned earlier, is extremely time-sensitive. To avoid such problems, Pfizer consistently hires its research directors from within.

DIFLUCAN: A BREAKTHROUGH DRUG

One of Pfizer's most memorable products—both scientifically and financially—is Diflucan, a drug that combats fungal infections. The story of its development illustrates the role of innovation at Pfizer and the element of serendipity in drug research.

In 1970, the company set out to develop a new class of drugs to fight the fungal infections that attack patients whose immune systems have been weakened by chemotherapy or organ transplants. The drugs that were already on the market caused terrible side effects, including the possibility of permanent kidney damage.

One of Pfizer's teams managed to remodel and improve the molecular structure of an existing antifungal medicine, but because the drug broke down so quickly once the patient ingested it, oral administration was out of the question. Another team developed a drug that was far more powerful than the available medications, but it caused birth defects in the offspring of test rats. It took over ten years of intensive research before Diflucan—powerful *and* safe—emerged in 1981. In high doses it cures severe fungal infec-

135

tions; in lower doses it cures athlete's foot and other minor infections.

And it was just that broad range of applicability that caused discord in Pfizer's top ranks. Should we develop Diflucan in the lower dosages to treat the lesser ailments? That, its proponents argued, would satisfy a much bigger market. Or should we develop it for high-dosage treatments, making a strong statement about its effectiveness and its very minor side effects? The faction that favored the high-dosage approach pointed out that helping cancer patients and the AIDS population with weakening immune systems had far greater medical significance and urgency than curing athlete's foot.

Neither side was willing to yield. Finally, we formed a team of talented people from various areas of the company, giving them explicit instructions to bring an end to the stand-off. We gave them no choice: We put them in a room and explained that nobody would leave until there was a plan that made sense for the whole company. In the end, the team designated the high-dosage approach, and I have no doubt that it made the right decision. We were so pleased with the team's performance that we institutionalized it as one of our advanced candidate management teams.

In the course of the twenty years between our first anti-fungal initiatives and Diflucan's approval by the FDA, the project passed through a thicket of false starts and misfortunes. At a particularly low point in the process, we discovered that only eighteen months earlier, a British company had patented a class of compounds similar to that used in Diflucan. In the end, however, Diflucan was a towering success. I guess it's fair to say that with every success come valuable lessons about the difficulty of predicting the course of invention and the importance of versatile management systems.

INNOVATION REWARDED

In my experience, and I doubt that anyone would disagree, the most productive scientists are the self-starters. They do their jobs well because being in a position to improve the human condition is what motivates them. And yet even though we understand that their motivation springs from internal sources, we at Pfizer reinforce their accomplishments and their self-esteem with pay increases and promotions for those who show leadership potential. We bestow gold stars as well: Pfizer Central Research Achievement Awards. We present these awards at two annual banquets, one in Groton, the other in Sandwich. Management and the research staff nominate about 1 percent of their peers each year.

Two aspects of the award program have played important parts in making it a success. First, the awards are not reserved solely for inventors of new drugs. For one thing, given our long development cycle and the odds against any single approach finding its way—unaltered—to market, identifiable inventors are few and far between. The team is really the basic research unit at Pfizer, and the forty-five people who receive the award each year are outstanding team players. In addition, we also reward insights—innovative discoveries—at critical junctures in the process of research.

We have, for example, recognized a clinician who described a new way to observe depressed patients. That new approach permitted us to understand the impact and potential new applications of one of our antidepressant drugs.

The other source of the award program's success is a function of the awards themselves. About ten years ago, when we first considered establishing the awards program, some of our managers maintained that unless there was a substantial amount of cash attached to the awards, people would consider them insignificant, and they would ridicule our stinginess.

Fortunately, those managers lost the argument. The award winners are thrilled by recognition from their peers and the management.

THE INTANGIBLES

As long as I have been involved in the pharmaceutical industry, I have realized that it is an industry obliged to impress a much broader audience than simply our end users. One of the peculiarities and challenges of the pharmaceutical trade is that truly effective innovators must address and impress a series of interested parties that includes physicians, health maintenance organizations (HMOs), regulatory agencies, and the larger public. Of course, it makes sense that companies that produce and profit from medications should be held to the highest standards. But it's not always easy to serve that many masters.

Obviously, therefore, we continuously look for fresh ways to improve our communications with those constituencies. Here's an example of a strategy that really worked for everyone involved.

The file drawers of virtually every general practitioner contain a certain number of "fat files." Those are the files of patients who have a wide variety of undifferentiated symptoms that usually include digestive distress and sleeplessness. Our experience tells us that most of those patients are suffering from chronic depression, but their doctors have failed to recognize the symptoms.

In 1992, Pfizer introduced Zoloft, an antidepressant drug. We knew that gaining market share was going to be an uphill struggle because Prozac had already established its commanding position. We developed several ancillary programs to support our marketing of Zoloft, and over time that medication has proven popular with patients and physicians. *Prime MD* was one of our most effective marketing innovations.

Prime MD comprises a series of tools and the only diagnostic kit clinically validated for use in recognizing depression. Pfizer distributes the kits to general practitioners in private practice, managed care facilities, and HMOs. Since *Prime MD*'s introduction in 1994, we have passed out tens of thousands of kits.

If more people suffering from depression get proper diagnosis and treatment, everyone benefits. The concurrent effect is a growing demand for antidepressants, and Pfizer shares in at least some of that growth. Our hope, obviously, is that the success of the kit will lead HMOs and physicians to include Zoloft on their approved list of antidepressants and perhaps recommend it.

Rhythms is another program we prepared for distribution to physicians. Many patients cherish the misconception that they can stop taking antidepressants when they start to feel better, after, say, a month. They simply pitch whatever remains in their prescription vials because they fail to understand that depression is a cyclical disease. Patients need to take all the medication their physicians prescribe, and that entire course ought to match federal guidelines, which suggest nine to twelve months.

Our *Rhythms* program provides educational materials for doctors to give to their patients at designated intervals. At a certain point in the process, for example, the *Rhythms* program reminds doctors to send their patients letters that urge them to take daily twenty-minute walks in addition to their continued medication.

When patients resume productive lives, everyone benefits: doctors, HMOs, and, of course, Pfizer. That is the value of programs like *Prime MD* and *Rhythms.* As in any business, the long-term winners are those that provide quality *and* value.

AND A LITTLE BIT OF LUCK

The thrust to innovate informs every aspect of business and life at Pfizer. We do everything we can to stimulate, organize, and direct creative development. That's how we control the innovation process and, as much as possible, keep it predictable. I say as much as possible because there is always the capricious variable of chance. The unpredictable always plays its part, but we have tried to institutionalize opportunism.

We caution our people not to wear blinders. They must avoid so totally immersing themselves in their specialties that they fail to recognize the significance of an unexpected finding. That's why our scientists are free to roam among disease areas and to follow leads wherever they go. We cannot discover tomorrow's drugs if we freeze everyone in rigid procedure.

Not long ago, Pfizer invested considerable energy and resources in a drug for treating hypertension. Tests indicated that its effects on hypertension were not all we had anticipated. That disappointment was offset by tests indicating that it would prove a much better treatment for arrhythmia—irregular heartbeat—than any other available medication. Another medicine, which was slated to treat anxiety, seems to be an extremely effective headache remedy.

On another occasion, our researchers were dissatisfied with the performance of a new medication we had developed to treat angina; it failed to alleviate angina's paroxysmal chest pains. Serendipity intervened, however, and defeat emerged as opportunity. By chance, we discovered the medication's extraordinary side effect: It restores sexual vigor to the impotent. The U.S. market for such a drug is significant. Impotence afflicts some 20 million men in this country alone.

As you no doubt have guessed, that particular revelation evoked a few raised eyebrows, and some of our competitors suggested that luck is perhaps our strongest suit. Those critics seem to have forgotten that it is always Pfizer's total commitment to innovation and creative change that prepares us to take advantage of stray pieces of good luck.

All in all, Pfizer's unique blend of partnerships, its commitment to speedy decision-making, its vast annals of research history (to which we constantly refer), and our flexible and versatile management systems enable us to spread power to all levels of our organization. With this in place, we are all at our innovative and creative best.

COMPANY PROFILE

PFIZER INC.

Business description	Research-based global health-care company
Founded	1849
Annual sales	$10.0 billion
Annual R&D expenditure	$1.7 billion
R&D as a percent of sales	17%

Net income before taxes	$2.3 billion
Net income after taxes	$1.6 billion
Number of employees worldwide	44,000
Number of employees in R&D	5,000

TOP PFIZER PRODUCTS

1940s

Penicillin

1950s

Terramycin (antibiotic)

1960s

Diabinese (for diabetes)

1970s

Minipress (for cardiovascular disease)

Sinequan (for central nervous system)

1980s

Feldene (anti-inflammatory)

Procardia XL (for cardiovascular disease)

1990s

Cardura (cardiovascular)

Glucotrol XL (metabolic/diabetes)

Norvasc (for cardiovascular disease)

Procardia XL (cardiovascular)

Zithromax (antibiotic)

Zoloft (for central nervous system)

The core of our strategy remains our determination to *innovate* our way through these demanding times. During the last fifteen years, our research and development (R&D) expenditures have grown at an average annual rate of almost 16 percent. . . .

Our commitment to innovative research has been rewarded. The combined performance of the six pharmaceuticals we most recently introduced in the U.S. contributed 58 percent to global pharmaceutical sales. For the first time in our history, three products—Norvasc, Zoloft, and Procardia XL—each achieved sales in excess of $1 billion.

William C. Steere, Jr., Chairman of the Board and Chief Executive Officer
1995 Annual Report

Fact: Pfizer products are available in more than 150 countries.

Fact: Fiscal 1995 was the 46th consecutive year in which Pfizer sales rose.

Fact: During World War I, when Pfizer scientists could no longer rely on a steady supply of lemons to make citric acid, they invented a method of producing it from sugar through deep-tank fermentation—a Pfizer first.

Fact: During World War II, Pfizer's expertise in fermentation technology permitted its scientists to pioneer the mass production of penicillin.

Fact: Terramycin, a Pfizer antibiotic, was one of the first broad-spectrum antibiotics. It was effective against bacteria that caused more than a hundred diseases.

Rubbermaid Inc.

"Technology paves the highway to perpetual innovation."

WOLFGANG SCHMITT
CHAIRMAN AND CHIEF EXECUTIVE OFFICER

Consumers and business cognoscenti alike have created a mystique around Rubbermaid. The professional-management press has ranked us among the top ten "most admired" companies for decades. Shoppers everywhere not only recognize our name; they can tell you exactly why they like our products. And what they like is precisely what we want them to like: Our products are useful; their quality is uncompromisingly high; and they are, therefore, a source of delight.

In an industry where corporate rivals do battle with products we charitably characterize as mundane—buckets, laundry baskets, kitchen containers, and the like—our accomplishments are unique. The prototypes of our products existed long before there was an industry to make them, and yet Rubbermaid continues to make products that distinguish themselves from the competition.

Nevertheless, our company has recently run into some rough weather. The price of resin—the basic element of production—has rapidly doubled, low-cost competitors have been giving us a buffeting, and our near-term sales and profitability have shown the strain. But Rubbermaid's fans and future remain steadfast. Our brands continue to prevail because of our persistent, consistently clever product innovation. As chairman and chief executive officer of Rubbermaid, I can tell you that we produce new forms of plastic molding nearly every day.

How do we sustain that hectic pace? We hew to the following powerful operating principles:

- Cross-functional teams are more reliably productive than any other organizational configuration.

- Oversight teams drawn from the company's top executives supervise every business unit.

- Company-wide business councils focus on performance and innovation in such business practices as marketing and design.

- We scrutinize market trends by keeping close watch on the surface activity and by digging well below its surface.

- In a competitive environment where speed-to-market makes the difference between success and failure, we waste neither time nor money on run-of-the-mill research. We spend money on design, production, inventory control, and wherever else innovation can have an immediate impact.

• By imposing creative tension, we inspire our people to come up with fresh solutions to new tasks in new environments.

• We offer every kind of training, but we leave it to the individual associate to take advantage of it.

Master of the mundane: That's how you might think of Rubbermaid. Our products solve the everyday problems that confront all people, of every culture, age, and economic status. Starting seventy-six years ago with a humble dustpan, Rubbermaid now offers more than five thousand different product solutions for home, office, play, and the great outdoors.

Each of our products reflects several generations of innovation, and innovation is what distinguishes Rubbermaid from a sea of competitors. Ingenuity of design to create the best combination of quality, price, timeliness, service, and innovation is our best defense against copycats and our best way to delight consumers.

In a marketplace where speed-to-market is critical, we don't do a lot of market testing or laborious intellectualizing about product development. If your notion of research and development has anything to do with scientists set apart in an ivory tower, don't look for Rubbermaid in that picture. Do you think our disdain for market testing is risky? Well, we are risk-takers who understand that it's batting average—not every turn at the plate—that counts. And our batting average is very good. We introduce some four hundred new products every year, and 80 percent of those products either meet or exceed their performance targets.

I attribute that remarkable record to both instinct and culture. We characterize our success as a combination of the Five Ts: trends, teams, training, technology, and creative tension.

We track trends because our success depends on our ability to tune into consumers' changing needs and expectations. We aim to translate our understanding of these into opportunities to delight consumers with solutions to their everyday problems. We've never met a trend we didn't like. Even those trends that seem negative at first blush often present opportunities for us to create a new way to solve a problem and achieve more quality growth.

Which trends do we consider? We track such conspicuous currents as demographic swings, changes in fashion, and market fluctuations, as well as the less apparent psychographic trends such as Information-Age symptoms and regulatory developments. Of course, the ideal outcome of those observations is the identification of an emerging trend, anticipation of consumers' needs, and solutions that come as a pleasant surprise to consumers and our customers alike.

Surprise is a distinctive feature of delight. Taking note of the public's desire to reduce waste, we developed a line of Litterless Lunch products: reusable sandwich containers, juice boxes, and lunch bags. Our introduction of that product line coincided fortuitously with Canadian regulations that require schoolchildren to bring litter-free lunches at least two days a week. Our Litterless Lunch Kit was an instant winner.

In many young families these days, both parents hold jobs outside the home, and domestically we are experiencing a steady boom of first births. As a result, recent years have witnessed continued growth in day care centers. We understood that those developments represented terrific opportunities for our juvenile-products business. The individuals who own or franchise most day care centers cannot afford to make large investments in playground equipment. Our Little Tikes unit responded to their need with the PlayCenter, a sturdy, mostly plastic playground structure. It's designed to handle lots of children, but it's eminently affordable.

Our affordable products respond to consumers' insistence on getting more for less. And yet many marketers have misunderstood the more-for-less expectation: People are not simply looking for the lowest price. Today's consumers are unwilling to sacrifice quality, service, or convenience for a good price. They expect—and Rubbermaid aims to deliver—it all.

The complexity of market trends creates the greatest number of opportunities for companies that embrace innovation. In the early years of our company, the typical Rubbermaid consumer was female, twenty-five to fifty years old, married, and staying at home to raise her children. Certainly it was easier to define our customers' needs in those days. Today's market is much more demanding and offers a broad diversity of opportunities.

We no longer assume, for example, that consumers for toolboxes are men. As a matter of fact, half of the people who purchase toolboxes are women, and it pays to know that. Because we learned that increasing numbers of women were doing home-improvement work, we introduced tool organizers in a new color, which we called Hardware Blue, kind of a royal-blue shade, which appeals to women and men alike. And today, that color outsells all others.

From color to product design to pricing, Rubbermaid's team-matrix structure balances our innovation groups' entrepreneurial approaches with their access to the resources of a $2.3-billion company. Every core team includes one member from each of four areas: marketing, design, finance, and manufacturing/engineering. An experienced product manager leads each of the teams.

The teams have global responsibility for their respective product lines—home organization, automotive, infant play, computer accessories, and so forth—and it's the cross-functional play that really makes them tick. Team members contribute from diverse perspectives to conceive, develop, price, and direct the marketing and merchandising of their products. Team heterogeneity promotes a good symmetry of design, engineering finesse, and marketing savvy that we might never achieve if we waited for isolated departments to bridge their efforts. Our teams work to optimize performance, profitability, development, and efficiency and thus ensure growth.

To encourage empowerment with accountability, an operating team composed of the general manager and the vice presidents of human resources, finance, marketing, R&D, and sales oversees each of our business units. And Rubbermaid's system of company-wide councils—for example, our marketing council—promotes best practices among our traditional functions. We assign a corporate officer to provide each council with strategic direction.

While it is true that we don't spend a lot of time doing pure scientific research, don't make the mistake of thinking we ignore current technology. Even our simplest items comprise an infusion of advanced techniques to achieve the best total value. An extensive array of computer-aided processes speed up virtually every aspect of our value chain: procuring materials from our suppliers; designing, modeling, and engineering our products; controlling such manufacturing particulars as how molten plastic should flow in our molds; tracking inventory and distribution; designing marketing and merchandising materials even before the first actual product has come off the machine; and monitoring retailers' scanner data to follow consumer purchases and continuously replenish our customers' inventories. We have, of course, invested heavily in information technologies, including an integrated system we're now putting into place to connect Rubbermaid's operations around the world and provide up-to-date data on everything from customer and vendor transactions to currency translations.

Learning to work with new systems and technologies can produce a certain amount of organizational tension, which is not always healthy. Creative tension within an organization is quite another matter. I encourage creative tension at Rubbermaid. I want our associates to channel their energies from the diversity of their experiences, values, and cultural norms into common creative directions. We organize our people into small teams whose members hail from distinctly different schools of thought, and those configurations spark creative energy.

Occasionally we try to stir up organizational creativity by challenging our staff with new assignments and changing roles. I sometimes tap a finance professional for the management of a marketing assignment, for example. New technologies also help people see new approaches to familiar tasks. We are always on the lookout for defenses against stagnancy. By keeping our responsibilities dynamic reflections of the changing environment—both internal and external—we will not get too comfortable with our current position. I work to keep that tension in careful balance with growth opportunities so that our people can continuously broaden their horizons. After all, as our associates expand their capabilities and fields of vision, they enhance their contributions to innovation.

Of course, none of that works well unless we invest in continuous learning. We cultivate a learning environment in which the sky's the limit. We encourage associates to log onto our internal networks to share information on process improvements, and through a variety of programs we provide opportunities for continuous education, which we expect of all associates. We believe it ignites individual initiative. Training opportunities are integrated within the working life of Rubbermaid. We also offer on-site MBA courses and language classes.

Our Five Ts—trends, teams, training, technology, and creative tension—give life to our culture of innovation, and innovation is, without a doubt, the most critical component of the value Rubbermaid and its people create. I expect every member of every team to make a personal commitment to superior performance and quality. Because there must be no doubt about Rubbermaid's commitment to superiority, we distribute a copy of our company's Statement of Management Philosophies to each associate who joins the company.

In addition to quality, our total-value focus extends, of course, to service and market performance. Salaries and bonuses rise and fall, and people win and lose assignments and responsibilities, all on the strength of their support for that standard. Here's an example.

Our research people define the composition of focus groups based on the nature of a particular product's consumer base. The focus group for laundry products is populated, for the most part, by women. The researchers provide the women with a Rubbermaid version of a particular product and ask them to compare it with a competitor's. After the women have had some experience using the competing products, we observe and record their reactions, eventually assembling the group to meet with the laundry team for discussion and evaluation of our would-be new product.

Because our laundry team has been so deeply involved in

the process, they can easily spot nuances of reaction that the uninitiated might miss. Some time ago, our team members noticed that the consumers in every group tended to carry laundry baskets on one hip, and because they invariably need to carry detergent as well, they were having some trouble balancing their loads. Perhaps you've found yourself trying to balance similarly awkward items. The basket refuses to rest comfortably on your hip, and your other arm—occupied with bottles, boxes, or both—is no help. More often than not, you need to retrace your steps to pick up those stray socks that seem to leap over the basket's edge.

Our laundry team's recognition and first-hand assessment of these problems led to Rubbermaid's Hip Hugger laundry basket, which joined our product line in 1995. Because the basket is kidney-shaped, it rests comfortably on one's hip.

But just having a well-designed product doesn't guarantee success. No invention sells itself. The world beats a path to your door only if people *know* about your better mousetrap. The next task for our laundry team was to convince merchants to display the baskets in a way that made the most of their unique shape.

The various team members applied their own expertise to the myriad facets of the basket's introduction. The team's finance and marketing members took responsibility for establishing its cost structure and pricing, and the team turned to the designer for such product specifications as the location of handles, shape and size, and colors in which to offer the product. But we also expect advantage from the cross-functional composition of our teams; experts who make only parochial contributions to their teams' deliberations are not full participants in the Rubbermaid development process.

THE BREAKTHROUGH PRODUCT

Where would we be if our teams contributed only product extensions? Recently a team in the seasonal products division introduced an entirely new notion: sturdy resin garden sheds. The sheds that team envisioned are already a multimillion-dollar product line.

That group noticed the limited options available to people who needed extra outdoor storage space. Their choices—from storage cabinets to makeshift sheds of aluminum or wood—were difficult to assemble and not all that durable.

In the meantime, our juvenile products business, Little Tikes, had for some time marketed a line of outdoor play houses, fashioned to look like cottages, log cabins, space stations, and castles. We had fitted their wall and roof panels with joints that simply snap together. Ever since we introduced those play houses, consumers have reported how much they appreciate the ease with which they can be put together, taken apart, and rebuilt.

Our seasonal products team applied that same logic to our new line of outdoor storage sheds. The team selected optimal manufacturing processes that let us mold the shed parts from durable resins. As expected, the team defined the details of packaging, shipping, and pricing. But the team made significantly innovative contributions, too. Its storage solutions offered more choices in sizes and pricing than anything already on the market; plastic made our sheds more durable and easier to handle than wood or metal sheds; and by importing and applying the snap-together logic, we were able to offer tool-free assembly.

The market responded to the sheds with enthusiasm. Customers are delighted that they can easily assemble their sheds in minutes. As a matter of fact, most people don't even need to read our instructions.

Those breakthrough sheds were possible because of our advances in plastic-molding technology, which we also use for our office products and furniture.

I should also point out that the often-ignored instruction sheets that come with those products don't rely on English or any other language. We use universally understood pictograms to communicate with consumers around the world. We believe that global utility, balanced with market-specific customization, is key to worldwide success. What do I mean by that? We know that consumers everywhere need wastebaskets. But we also recognize the range of wastebaskets that serve the world. In certain parts of the world, for example, a thirty-two-gallon trash can is just too big to be useful—especially for a family in a five hundred-square-foot flat. And unlike North American consumers, who have no problem with open trash cans, Europeans have no use for a trash can that doesn't have a tight-fitting lid. In Europe, open garbage is considered downright unhygienic.

In every market, though, innovation is a must. Depending

on one's job, innovation has many meanings at Rubbermaid. For staff in such a service area as finance, innovation means faster or more efficient collection processes. On the product-marketing side, innovation might involve promotional approaches that really make a difference.

Channels for marketing are also important. Back in the 1950s and 1960s party-plan businesses sold household gadgets, toys, and cosmetics to consumers right in their homes. Today's aggressive work schedules have limited the amount of time consumers spend in their homes, and Rubbermaid has taken the number-one position in the North American housewares business. Consumers now turn to discount stores, supermarkets, and home centers for those products. We have succeeded by selling our products wherever consumers want to shop.

Public response to our Servin' Saver food containers has always been positive because their tight seals keep food fresh, and the containers survive repeated trips from the freezer into the microwave and through the dishwasher cycle. As popular as the Servin' Savers were, however, the tight seal was difficult to open for children and people afflicted with arthritis. Our response, an award-winning line of containers called EZ Topps, seal just as well as the original line, but their lids have a tab for easy opening.

Although that was a simple innovation, it had far-reaching impact, and it exemplifies our total value approach. With a small but targeted product change we were able to make a big difference with consumers.

Price is another factor critical to consumers. A fair price is a price that reflects a product's quality, innovative features, and competitive position. Competitors copy such household basics as our old-fashioned laundry basket and ordinary coolers. We price such products very competitively with the visual knockoffs. On the other hand, we can sell our Hip Hugger laundry basket and four-wheeled ice chest at a higher price because consumers value their special features.

As our industry's innovation leader, we are reconciled to seeing many of our products copied or, like ice cube trays, turned into commodities. Buckets, wastebaskets, food storage containers, and the like are easily duplicated with injection molding. That's why we at Rubbermaid always look for ways to differentiate our product lines.

EZ Topps, for example, extended our original line of Servin' Savers. Realistically, we knew as soon as we introduced them that we'd soon see competitors' versions appearing with levers and tabs, but because our EZ Topps were first, we established a preeminent position on retailers' shelves. Retail shelf space is valuable, and we work to win that space by getting our best ideas to market fast and first. Our customers responded to EZ Topps with enthusiasm and requests for more varieties.

Although we have aggressively defended our innovations in court—and we will continue to do so—in the final analysis, we prefer to play offense rather than defense. We keep our sights trained on our process of continuous innovation.

RIDING THE TRENDS

Whatever turns out to be our next breakthrough, I can guarantee that it will reflect changing trends, providing a one-to-one solution for the consumer on a mass-market scale. Remember the Litterless Lunch juice box I mentioned earlier? Its introduction was a brilliant reflection of consumer interest in conservation and the environment. It looks like the paper juice boxes you've seen, but we make it out of reusable plastic with a screw-on top and a sturdy, reusable straw that couples with a special seal in the top. Parents appreciate that. It's tidier than paper juice boxes, which offer no sealing mechanism for the straw. Give the disposable versions a squeeze when the straw is in place and you'll see what I mean.

Not long ago, Rubbermaid founded a Health Care Products unit with our acquisition of Carex, a leader in home health-care items. Hospital stays are getting shorter, and more and more people receive treatment and other health care in their own homes. These are trends that spell opportunity.

As we examined consumers' experiences with home health care along with patients' desires to maintain their self-reliance, we discovered that the market had neglected certain areas that meshed with our resources and abilities. End users informed us that such currently available products as walkers, canes, bath benches, and bed trays were neither ergonomically designed nor attractively priced. In fact, we found that the designs for many of those products had not been revisited since their introduction to the market in the '50s and '60s. With lots of chrome and hinges, they had the cold look and feel of a hospital ward. They were heavy and cumbersome, and especially in the case of walkers, the metal made them uncomfortable to use.

We anticipated a welcoming market for products that don't make patients' homes look like hospital wards. Ergonomics, we knew, would play an important part in the product-design process. We aimed to replace a good portion of the metal and heavy materials with lightweight, strong, and durable plastics.

We replaced the hard rubber handles on walkers as soon as we saw that users tried to cushion the handles by wrapping them with towels. When we unveiled models for Rubbermaid's new version of the walker, consumers responded well to the built-in spongy hand grips, easy-fold mechanism, anchor hooks for food trays, and front pocket for cordless phones. To meet consumer demand, we began to expand our distribution beyond medical supply dealers to include drugstores and other retail outlets. All of this was in direct response to trends in home health care.

Consumers themselves keep us posted on current trends, but we also track media events, political developments, social shifts, economic changes, and grassroots movements. I believe that associates at every level, and in every job, can learn to be "trend messengers." Trend messengers gather information from the world around them and share their observations with the rest of our organization.

Our people are encouraged to search out angles and opportunities from the information that confronts them both on and off the job. We want them to raise questions, offer challenges, and share their observations. And our teams consider the accumulation of their colleagues' musings and observations with the ultimate goal of unearthing new product ideas.

COMPUTER-AIDED EVERYTHING

Technology paves the highway to perpetual innovation. I consider computer-aided design, computer-aided engineering, computer-aided manufacturing—computer-aided everything—the crucial tools of Rubbermaid's progress.

Using computer models, we define our products' physical properties and specifications, test their structural integrity, and develop the packaging, including photographically realistic images of products still under development. Our aggressive use of technology allows us to dispatch our sales force even before we have actual products to show the retailers. And our extensive computer networks allow our research and development people, suppliers, marketing staff, manufacturing experts, sales staff, distributors, retail customers, and even consumers to contribute to our total value process.

Our quest for superior value in everything Rubbermaid does incorporates a philosophy of continuous improvement. We strive always to make things happen efficiently, effectively, and fast.

RUBBERMAID'S TOTAL VALUE PROCESS:
STIRRING THINGS UP

The Rubbermaid goal is to sustain and harness an atmosphere of perpetual creative energy. And it's my job to continually stir calming waters. For people who are uncomfortable in a changeable environment, the benefits of ongoing evolution aren't always apparent. But we work hard to make certain that our associates understand that change is Rubbermaid's constant, and people's roles are never static.

Our dynamic culture rewards enthusiasm for innovation and transformation. Like many other successful companies, we have long recognized that people will eschew risk-taking unless they understand that there are no penalties for experiments that fail. Some lessons are valuable simply for what we can learn from them.

Occasionally we need to redirect our course, and that may appear inefficient. Such upheaval does engender innovation, however, and that's how we earn our return on excitement. Rubbermaid innovators are rewarded with more opportunities to reach further for star status. But even that's not a big deal. We expect everyone to achieve their own potential for star status.

Do my expectations seem strange or unrealistic? Perhaps. I know that our challenge is to find and keep people who have the confidence to take business risks. Stagnation and fear are our worst enemies.

Let me illustrate what I mean. Last December marked a Rubbermaid milestone: our Global Leadership Development

Program graduated its first class of new hires who had on-the-job-training on our company business teams. The three-year-old program brings people from diverse cultures around the world into our midst. It's part of our strategy for globalizing Rubbermaid from the inside out. We recognize that to sell products to the world, our workforce must mirror the world.

Each of the associates who enrolls in our Global Leadership program speaks excellent English, and most of them have already earned MBAs in the United States or Great Britain. They start in entry-level management positions, and we move them from one assignment to another as they gain new levels of experience. As they acquire a broad range of skills from different parts of Rubbermaid's operations, we take the opportunity to assess where we can make the most of their talents. We assign them to cross-functional teams, or sales, or a start-up location outside the United States.

We undertook that program because we realized that we needed to diversify our internal culture—a culture primarily American in tradition. Rubbermaid needs to find new ways to approach problems. The international background of the program participants will help us consider different ways to market our products around the world. This way, we not only broaden our cultural experience and gain fresh perspectives, we also improve the company's business position worldwide.

Many of our domestic facilities are located in small towns, and some of our associates were uncomfortable with the Global Leadership Development Program. Its international nature produced tensions. Long-time employees asked us, "Who is this person from a strange nation? Why do I have to deal with them? They know nothing about our business, and I'm supposed to train them so they can help make us a global company?" And my response is an unequivocal "Yes." We are planting the germ of internationalism, hoping that it will take hold and spread throughout the body corporate.

We know that consumers respect organizational diversity, and we work to ensure that our magazine and catalog advertising depicts people who reflect the world. We want our products to reflect diversity as well. That's why we designed Little Tikes toys to accommodate children who can't walk or who have limited mobility.

Our new Push 'n' Ride Coupe toy exemplifies that effort. Its push-bar extension and removable floorboard make it easy for a person to push a child who—for whatever reason—can't walk. Our job at Rubbermaid is to make sure that our products respond to our customers' extensive and varied range of concerns, cultures, and characteristics.

DOWN-TO-EARTH RESEARCH

In keeping with our commitment to provide superior value, our research laboratories direct their attention to the very specific concerns of our customers. Business teams from our Commercial Products division, for instance, regularly spend time with restaurant owners who use such Rubbermaid products as serving and cleanup containers, high chairs, and cooking utensils. Team members actually flip burgers and bus

tables in order to gain real—and sometimes gritty—experien-
tial data. During a stint working in a restaurant kitchen, one
of our teams saw that the chef preferred to use synthetic-rub-
ber scrapers instead of metal spatulas whenever he cooked in
no-stick pans. The synthetic rubber didn't scrape the pans'
surfaces, but after repeated use, the scrapers warped and lost
their shape. The result of that discovery was a new High Heat
Scraper made of pliable synthetic rubber. Designed with professional chefs in mind, the new scraper can withstand tem-
peratures up to 500 degrees Fahrenheit without melting.

Such on-the-spot research is particularly valuable to our
retail customers. To be successful, they need to know how to
merchandise our products: the appropriate pricing, the most
popular colors, and so forth. Retailers need to make the most
of their limited shelf space, and our research gives them the
key to their customers' buying power.

Our Everything Rubbermaid lab stores are substantive
sources to help us meet and exceed our retailers' expectations. We use the stores to test the effectiveness of various
merchandising methods, and we share the results of those
experiments with retailers. We might, for instance, run a test
involving two laundry basket models—one big, one small—
priced the same. Our object in such a test would be to determine whether the big basket's sales rose because shoppers
considered it a better bargain than the smaller basket. We
structure such tests in any number of ways, and our results
are useful to improving our retailers' productivity.

As I mentioned previously, recent observations of shoppers revealed that both women and men were buying tool-boxes, power-tool cases, and other workshop organizers. We didn't know whether the women were buying the items for men or for themselves, but we knew for sure that the increase in female buyers was meaningful. It was time, we knew, to take a fresh look at our hardware line. We had been offering products in three colors—yellow, gray, and black—and we thought perhaps it was time to test other colors.

The color we call Hardware Blue is the upshot of our focus group research. I certainly wouldn't characterize it as a feminine color, but women in our focus groups did respond positively to it. Our next step was to see how the Hardware Blue boxes performed in our Everything Rubbermaid stores. Not only did Hardware Blue immediately outsell other colors, we were pleased to discover that it appealed just as strongly to men as to women. Our retailers were glad to have that information when they purchased their new stock: Knowledge, after all, reduces risk.

DEDICATION AND DELIGHT

When the cost of plastic resin, our major raw material, doubled in less than a year, it affected our short-term financial results. One decision we had to consider was where to cut back, at least temporarily. Sure, we could have cut some training investments. But it's my belief that we should not dilute our commitment to those activities, because like our globalization and technological programs, training programs are the fuel of our long-term quality growth.

People—especially other businesspeople—often ask me how Rubbermaid sustains its success in consistent innovation. Here's the short answer: Rubbermaid's policy, continually expressed and vigorously pursued, is to *delight* consumers and customers. Do you think I'm being frivolous or fanciful when I speak of invoking consumer delight? Believe it or not, our entire organization is focused on achieving delight. People who do laundry tell us they are delighted with the hip-hugger laundry basket. Retailers tell us they are delighted with our value-added services in merchandising and marketing. Our help drives retail sales, attracting buyers. Retail customers and consumers alike are delighted with our selection of more than five thousand products. None of our competitors even comes close to matching that. To customers, we mean one-stop shopping for a variety of outstanding products. To consumers, we mean quality solutions that are an outstanding value.

Our pride in achieving delight is a source of continuing inspiration and the font of Rubbermaid's innovation.

COMPANY PROFILE

RUBBERMAID INC.

Business description	Consumer-product manufacturing company
Founded	1920
Annual sales	$2.3 billion
Annual R&D Expenditure	$30,000
R&D as a percent of sales	not available
Net income before realignment	$158.5 million

Net income after taxes	$60 million
Number of employees worldwide	14,000
Number of employees in R&D	not available

TOP TRADEMARKS OF RUBBERMAID AND ITS SUBSIDIARIES

2-in-1 Wagon

Action Packer

Anything Goes

Aspira

Better workspace for the work place

Contours

Cozy Coupe

Elegance

Euro Blue

Expressions

EZMT

EZ Topps

Fresh Tops

Fun that Lasts

Graco

Grand Mansion

Grand Mansion Collectibles

Grip Liner

Ice Designs

Little Tikes

Lunch Break

OfficeWorks

Omni

Peek-A-Boo Activity Tunnel

Peninsula Table

Professional Plus

Rubbermaid

Safety Stripes

SimpliFile

Slide n'Stack

SnapEase

Toys That Last

UFO-User Friendly Office

In our seventy-five years, from making toy balloons to storage sheds, the difference between the present and the past has been punctuated by creative new ideas. Now, more than ever, customers and consumers around the globe demand more for less. It sets the stage for proficient, competitive marketing and exciting opportunities, and clearly, those who don't have the ideas to embrace the future are destined to become part of the past.

Wolfgang R. Schmitt, Chairman of the Board and Chief Executive Officer and Charles A. Carroll, President and Chief Operating Officer 1995 Annual Report

Our vision statement says we plan to grow as a global enterprise by developing best values through innovation.

And innovation is more than a word at Rubbermaid; it is a way of life. It is innovation that enables us to create products which are responsive to consumer trends and which make life more productive and enjoyable, thus delivering our promise.

Wolfgang R. Schmitt, Chairman and Chief Executive Officer
1994 Annual Meeting Address

Fact: Since 1994, the company has introduced, on average, one new product every day.

RECENT AWARDS AND HONORS

- Outdoor Storage Shed Program of Rubbermaid Specialty Products, Inc. was selected one of the outstanding products at the 1996 National Hardware Show.

- Pro Series Double Deep Tackle Box of Rubbermaid Specialty Products, Inc. was awarded Best of Show at the 1996 International ASA Sportfishing Expo in the Tackle Box Category.

- EZ Topps Food Containers won the 1996 Good Buy Award, presented to innovative products that solve everyday consumer problems, and the 1995 TYLENOL/Arthritis Foundation Design Award in the Kitchen/Household Products category

- In 1995, Rubbermaid Specialty Products, Inc. won the Silver Hammer Award from *National Home Center News* for Outstanding Marketing in the Lawn & Garden/Outdoor Equipment category.

- Rubbermaid's Home Products Division won the 1995 First Place SPARC (Supplier Performance Award by Retail Category).

- Little Tikes Co. sold more than 840,000 of its child-sized vehicles in 1995—more vehicles than either Honda or Ford.

- The Cozy Coupe Car sold more than 400,000 units in 1995—more than Honda Accord or Ford Taurus.

- Little Tikes Co. was named Toys "R" Us Partner of the Year in 1995, the retailer's highest honor.

About the Editors

ROSABETH MOSS KANTER

Rosabeth Moss Kanter holds the Class of 1960 Chair as Professor of Business Administration at the Harvard Business School. Her latest book, *World Class: Thriving Locally in the Global Economy*, about the impact of globalization on businesses, workplaces, and communities, was published by Simon & Schuster in September 1995. It shows how "collaborative advantage" produces success in the new economy.

She also wrote *When Giants Learn to Dance: Mastering the Challenges of Strategy, Management and Careers in the 1990s* (1989), which received the Johnson, Smith & Knisely Award for New Perspectives on Executive Leadership and was translated into ten languages. Other books include *The*

Challenge of Organizational Change (1992), *The Change Masters: Innovation and Entrepreneurship in the American Corporation* (1983), and *Men and Women of the Corporation* (1977), winner of the C. Wright Mills Award for the year's best book on social issues. She has published 12 books in total and over 150 articles. "Best article" awards include a McKinsey Award from the *Harvard Business Review.*

Before joining the Harvard Business School faculty, Professor Kanter taught at Brandeis and Harvard universities (1967–1977) and at Yale University (1977–1986). She was also a fellow in Law and Social Sciences and a Visiting Scholar at Harvard Law School. She co-founded Goodmeasure, Inc., a consulting firm, in 1977, serving as Chairman for the last eighteen years and producing *A Tale of "O": On Being Different,* one of the world's best-selling videos on workplace diversity. From 1989 to 1992 Professor Kanter was also Editor of the *Harvard Business Review,* which was a finalist for a National Magazine Award for General Excellence in 1991.

Professor Kanter has received numerous national honors, including a Guggenheim Fellowship, eighteen honorary doctoral degrees, and several Woman of the Year awards. She has been a consultant to major corporations all over the world, including Bell Atlantic and Hughes in the United States, Volvo and Inmarsat in Europe, Lippo Group and San Miguel in Asia. She has served on government commissions on economic issues, including innovation and entrepreneurship, employee involvement, and takeover laws, and is currently on the Board of Overseers for the Malcolm Baldrige National Quality Award and on the Massachusetts Governors Council on Economic Growth and Technology, co-chairing the task force on international trade. She is also on the boards of public interest organizations such as City Year and Alliance for the Commonwealth.

Professor Kanter was featured in the nationally broadcast American television special "Quality or Else" (1991–1992) and was the subject of two prime-time television documentaries on the leadership of change by the BBC (British Broadcasting Corporation) in 1988 and 1990. She hosts *Rosabeth Moss Kanter on Synergies, Alliances, and New Ventures* in the Harvard Business School Video Series and a new HBS Best Practices video series, *Partnering*.

JOHN KAO

John Kao, an authority on the new economy, specializes in the intersecting fields of corporate creativity, new media/information technology, and entrepreneurial management. He is the author of the recent best-selling book *Jamming: The Art and Discipline of Business Creativity,* which has been published in twenty languages worldwide. Trained in both psychiatry (Yale and Harvard medical schools) and business (Harvard Business School), he is an author and lecturer who also practices what he preaches.

Kao is academic director of the Managing Innovation executive program at Stanford University. For the past fourteen years, he was a professor at the Harvard Business

School, where he taught courses in the MBA and Advanced Management programs. He also created and served as Program Chair for the HBS executive program *Enhancing Corporate Creativity.* He was visiting professor at the MIT Media Lab from January to June of 1996. He has also taught at Yale University, the University of Copenhagen, and the Stanford Graduate School of Business.

His publications include the monograph *Entrepreneurship, Creativity and Organization* (1989) and the book series *Managing Creativity, The Entrepreneur,* and *The Entrepreneurial Organization,* all published in 1991 by Prentice Hall. He is also author of the widely read *Harvard Business Review* article "The Worldwide Web of Chinese Business" (1993). He has been quoted widely in such business publications as the *Wall Street Journal, Fortune,* and *The Economist.*

Kao is a member of the Global Business Network and a Fellow of the World Economic Forum. He is Chief Executive Officer of The Idea Factory, a company defining the state of the art in corporate creativity through the use of advanced training methods, computer/multimedia software, and value-added computer networks. He has founded several other companies, including Genzyme Tissue Repair (a public company involved with advanced tissue engineering), K.O. Technology (next-generation cancer diagnostics and therapeutics), and Pacific Artists (feature film production). He served as Chair of the 45th International Design Conference in Aspen, which took up the challenge of reframing design in light of the new needs of business. He has also served as adviser to many companies in fields such as biotechnology, entertainment, computer software, and financial services.

Kao maintains an interest in feature films. He was a production executive on *sex, lies and videotape*, which won the Palme d'Or (First Prize) at the 1989 Cannes Film Festival. He was also executive producer of *Mr. Baseball*, a Fred Schepisi film starring Tom Selleck that was financed and distributed by MCA/Universal. Kao is currently working on several feature film projects and has just directed a feature-length film based on *Jamming*. In his spare time, he plays jazz piano.

FRED WIERSEMA

Fred Wiersema is a business strategist and sought-after lecturer whose thought-provoking insights have captivated managers around the world. He is the founder of Ibex Partners, which specializes in strategic and management team alignment.

Before starting his own firm, he was a Senior Vice President at CSC Index, an international management consultancy. There, he initiated the firm's market leadership practice and co-authored *The Discipline of Market Leaders* (1995). That book quickly became a *New York Times* bestseller, appeared on the *Business Week* best-seller list for seventeen straight months (including five months in the number-one spot), and was translated into sixteen languages. His latest book, *Customer Intimacy* (1996), dissects the latest practices of companies that pursue this most promising customer value strategy.

He has consulted with Apple, EMI Music, Ford, Kraft USA, McDonald's, Xerox, and a host of others—including dozens of entrepreneurial firms—on issues ranging from streamlining and channel management, to competitive positioning and executive alignment. Earlier, he was in senior account management with J. Walter Thompson advertising, held executive positions with two high-tech ventures, and was a professor of business strategy and marketing at Simmons Graduate School of Management.

Dr. Wiersema was born in the Netherlands. He holds a doctorate in business administration from Harvard Business School, a master's in marketing from the University of Lancaster, England, and a bachelor's degree in economics from Erasmus University in Rotterdam. He and his family live in the Boston area.

Index